ESSENTIAL HISTORIES

CAESAR'S CIVIL WAR 49–44 BC

Adrian Goldsworthy

OSPREY PUBLISHING
Bloomsbury Publishing Plc
Kemp House, Chawley Park, Cumnor Hill, Oxford OX2 9PH, UK
29 Earlsfort Terrace, Dublin 2, Ireland
1385 Broadway, 5th Floor, New York, NY 10018, USA
E-mail: info@ospreypublishing.com
www.ospreypublishing.com

OSPREY is a trademark of Osprey Publishing Ltd

First published in Great Britain in 2023

The text in this edition is revised and updated from: ESS 42: *Caesar's Civil War: 49–44 BC*
(Osprey Publishing, 2002).
Essential Histories Series Editor: Professor Robert O'Neill

A catalogue record for this book is available from the British Library.

ISBN: PB 9781472855077;
eBook 9781472855060;
ePDF 9781472855053;
XML 9781472855084

23 24 25 26 27   10 9 8 7 6 5 4 3 2 1

Cover, page design and layout by Stewart Larking
In reference to the image on page 75 of this book: Istenič, Janka,
ROMAN MILITARY EQUIPMENT FROM THE RIVER
LJUBLJANICA. Typology, Chronology and Technology.
Catalogi et monographiae 43, Ljubljana 2019, p. 261, fig. A1.1a.
Maps by The Map Studio, revised by J B Illustrations
Index by Zoe Ross
Printed and bound in India by Replika Press Private Ltd.

Osprey Publishing supports the Woodland Trust, the UK's leading
woodland conservation charity.

To find out more about our authors and books visit
www.ospreypublishing.com. Here you will find
extracts, author interviews, details of forthcoming
events and the option to sign up for our newsletter.

CONTENTS

PROLOGUE

Julius Caesar remains famous to this day, even though the Classics no longer play much role in education. He is remembered as a statesman, as a great soldier, as the lover of Cleopatra, and because of Shakespeare's play (even though he is murdered early in Act 3 and the real tragic hero of the play is Brutus). Journalists use expressions like 'Crossing the Rubicon', 'The die is cast', or 'The Ides of March', confident that the references will be sufficiently understood to make their point. All three refer to moments covered in this book.

Caesar was widely considered the most successful commander in Rome's history, with Pliny the Elder noting that he fought and won more battles than anyone else, although also lamenting the heavy death toll resulting from his campaigns. Yet like all Roman commanders until Late Antiquity, Caesar was not a full-time soldier, but a politician following a career in public life that brought him civil as well as military posts. In his youth he spent little time with the army, although he managed to win an award for bravery, the *corona civica*, in his late teens and gave hints of immense self-confidence. At the age of 39 he was appointed to govern one of Rome's Spanish provinces and from then on until his death in his 56th year, his life was dominated by warfare in way that had never been true before. Thus, the battles Pliny mentions were all fought in this last period of his life and it was then that he forged his reputation as a military genius. Hindsight means that we do not find any of this surprising, but like Alexander or Napoleon or Lee we come to his campaigns expecting to see signs of immense talent and knowing that as military leaders these men were special. At the time, Romans, and especially other senators, had no reason to expect that Caesar would overrun Gaul so rapidly. Even after this, they may have wondered whether Caesar and his army would match up so well against disciplined opponents, let alone against the proven talent of Pompey. Whatever their feelings about Caesar and his cause, relatively few senators shared Caelius Rufus' opinion that he had the better army and was much more likely to win. Far more of them placed their trust in Pompey's record, and, after his death, in the prestige of the remaining commanders, or preferred to remain neutral.

Caesar was not simply a great general, but a remarkably fluent writer and it is well known that the bulk of our evidence for his campaigns comes from his own *Commentaries*. (In the case of the Civil Wars, we are a little better off as from the end of 48 BC the accounts of the remainder of the conflict were written by others after Caesar's death, albeit by men who had served under him and were admirers). Many generals would surely envy this, although few men of action have matched Caesar's skill with words – Churchill is an obvious exception, but there are not many others. Overtly dispassionate, referring to himself in the third person, and often vague about his own activities, allowing readers – or at the time often listeners, since books were expensive and public readings common – to imagine for themselves appropriately heroic actions, the *Commentaries* combine pacy storytelling with self-serving propaganda. Whatever the details, the overwhelming impression is that when Caesar was present – or his influence most obviously felt – the right decisions were made and his men fought with an unsurpassed skill and heroism as true Romans. That critics of individual decisions or of Caesar's generalship more widely have found plenty of ammunition in his own narrative, let alone reading between the lines of his account, highlights its essential honesty, but also its subtlety. Allowing the reader to see apparent misjudgements only reinforces the overall sense of immense ability and the undoubted ultimate success.

However we judge Caesar as a commander, the simple truth remains that he did keep winning, and that setbacks like Dyrrachium did not turn into catastrophic defeats. He never lost a war, and his ultimate failure

OPPOSITE
A coin minted during Caesar's dictatorship, showing him wearing the laurel wreath of a triumphing general. The right to wear this on all public occasions helped to conceal his receding hairline. (akg-images)

was political, misreading the mood of the senators who conspired against him. The campaigns described in this book were all civil wars, with the exception of the Zela campaign and Alexandria, although there many of his opponents were former Roman soldiers in service of the Ptolemies. Civil war plagued Rome's Republic from 88 to 31 BC, as it would later plague the Roman Empire from the 3rd century AD until the final collapse in the West in AD 476. The impact of these Roman against Roman clashes on the development of the army is rarely considered, so it is worth reminding ourselves that the last five years of Caesar's life, and many of his hardest campaigns, were waged against armies led by men he knew well, following the same doctrines and tactics.

Hard though it for us to take in, almost none of Rome's civil wars was fought over matters of ideology. The war following Caesar's death is a partial exception, even though Brutus and Cassius quickly started to behave just like the other warlords of the era, bribing their men to keep their loyalty. These were conflicts about personal prestige and power, and, as Pliny noted, they caused immense suffering. Large parts of the Mediterranean world were plundered as the rival armies faced off against each other. Caesar felt justified fighting the war to protect his honour and status – they wanted it, as he declared after Pharsalus. At the same time those opponents saw their own determination to end his career as equally justified. Yet many of those caught up in the conflict had little choice in the matter. Militarily the war is interesting because of the wide variety of situations it created, and the relentless, aggressive and flexible way that it was fought, especially by Caesar. Politically it mattered, because Caesar's victory and subsequent murder set the scene for the rise of the man who would become Caesar Augustus and create a regime that established the rule of emperors and did so much to shape Western culture.

INTRODUCTION

The Roman Republic and its growing problems

Although originally a monarchy, Rome had become a Republic near the end of the 6th century BC. Such political revolutions were commonplace in the city-states of the ancient world, but after this Rome proved remarkably stable, free from the often violent internal disputes that constantly beset other communities. Gradually at first, the Romans expanded their territory, and by the beginning of the 3rd century BC they controlled virtually all of the Italian peninsula. Conflict with Carthage, which began in 265 (all dates are BC unless stated otherwise) and continued sporadically until that city was utterly destroyed in 146, resulted in the acquisition of overseas provinces. By this time Rome dominated the entire Mediterranean world, having defeated with ease the successor kingdoms which had emerged from the break-up of Alexander the Great's empire.

Roman expansion continued, and time and time again its legions were successful in foreign wars, never losing a conflict even if they sometimes suffered defeat in individual battles. Yet, the stability and unity of purpose which had so characterised Roman political life for centuries began to break down. Politicians started to employ violent means to achieve their ends, the disputes escalating until they became civil wars fought on a massive scale. A succession of charismatic military leaders emerged, men able to persuade their soldiers to fight other Romans. In 49 Julius Caesar, faced with the choice between being forced out of politics altogether or starting a civil war, invaded Italy. His success effectively tolled the death knell of the Republican political system, for after his victory he established himself as sole ruler of the Roman world. Caesar was murdered because his power was too blatant, and the assassination returned

Rome to another period of civil war, which ended only when Caesar's nephew and adopted son Octavian defeated his last rival in 31. It was left to Octavian, later given the name Augustus, to create the regime known as the Principate, a monarchy in all but name, returning stability to Rome and its empire at the cost of a loss of political freedom.

The Roman republican system was intended to prevent any individual or group within the state from gaining overwhelming and permanent power. The Republic's senior executive officers or magistrates, the most senior of whom were the two consuls, held power (*imperium*) for a single year, after which they returned to civilian life. A mixture of custom and law prevented any individual being elected to the same office in successive years, or at a young age, and in fact it was rare for the consulship to be held more than twice by any man. Former magistrates, and the pick of the wealthiest citizens in the state formed the Senate, a permanent council which advised the magistrates and also supervised much of the business of government, for instance, despatching and receiving embassies. The Senate also chose the province (which at this period still meant sphere of responsibility and only gradually was acquiring fixed geographical associations) to be allocated to each magistrate, and could extend the *imperium* of a man within the same province for several years.

Roman politics was fiercely competitive, as senators pursued a career that brought them both civil and military responsibilities, sometimes simultaneously. It was very rare for men standing for election to advocate any specific policies, and there was nothing in any way equivalent to modern political parties within the Senate. Each aristocrat instead tried to represent himself as a capable man, ready to cope with whatever task the Republic required of him, be it leading an army or building an aqueduct. Men paraded their past achievements and – since often before election they personally had done little – the achievements of past generations of their family. Vast sums of money were lavished on the

OPPOSITE
Unlike Caesar, Augustus was not a great general. However, he had the knack of finding able subordinates and making sure their success was attributed to him. (Photo By DEA / A. DAGLI ORTI/De Agostini via Getty Images)

electorate, especially in the form of games, gladiator shows, feasts and the building of great monuments. This gave great advantages to a small core of established and exceptionally wealthy families who as a result tended to dominate the senior magistracies. In the 1st century there were eight praetorships (senior magistracies of lower ranking than consulships), and even more of the less senior posts, but still only ever two consulships. This meant that the majority of the 600 senators would never achieve this office. The higher magistracies and most of all the consulship offered the opportunity for the greatest responsibilities and therefore allowed men to achieve the greatest glory, which enhanced their family name for the future. The consuls commanded in the most important wars, and in Rome military glory always counted for more than any other achievement. The victor in a great war was also likely to profit from it financially, taking a large share of the booty and the profits from the mass enslavement of captured enemies. Each senator strove to serve the Republic in a greater capacity than all his contemporaries. The propaganda of the Roman elite is filled with superlatives, each man striving to achieve bigger and better deeds than anyone else, and special credit was attached to being the first person to perform an act or defeat a new enemy. Aristocratic competition worked to the Republic's advantage for many generations, for it provided a constant supply of magistrates eager to win glory on the state's behalf.

However, in the late 2nd century BC the system began to break down. Rome had expanded rapidly, but the huge profits of conquest had not been distributed evenly, so a few families benefited enormously. The gap between the richest and poorest in the Senate widened, and the most wealthy were able to spend lavishly to promote their own and their family's electoral success. It became increasingly expensive to pursue a political career, a burden felt as much by members of very old but now modestly wealthy families as by those outside the political elite. Such men could only succeed by borrowing vast sums of money, hoping to repay these

debts once they achieved the highest offices. The risk of failure, which would thus bring financial as well as political ruin, could make such men desperate. At the same time men from the richest and most prestigious families saw opportunities to have even more distinguished careers than their ancestors by flouting convention and trying to build up massive blocks of supporters. Both types were inclined to act as *populares*, an abusive term employed by critics to signify men who appealed to the poorer citizens for support by promising them entertainment, subsidised or free food, or grants of land. The *popularis* was an outsider, operating beyond the bounds of and with methods unattractive to the well-established senators. It was a very risky style of politics, but one which potentially offered great opportunities. In 133 a radical tribune – the ten tribunes of the plebs were magistrates without military responsibilities who were supposed to protect the interests of the people – from one of the most prestigious families, Tiberius

Underneath the palace of the Emperor Domitian on the Palatine Hill lies a 1st century BC house. A good deal of politics took place in aristocrats' houses. (Author)

Sempronius Gracchus, was lynched by a mob of senators when he tried to gain re-election to a second year of office. In 121, his brother Caius, who pursued an even more radical agenda, was killed by his opponents in something that came close to open fighting in the very centre of Rome. Yet a small number of men began to have previously unimaginable electoral success, as many of the old precedents restricting careers were broken. From 104 to 100, a successful general named Caius Marius was elected to five successive consulships.

In the same period the conversion of the Roman army into a professional force fundamentally altered its relationship with the rest of society. Until this time the legions had been militia forces, all citizens who possessed a certain property qualification being obliged to serve when called upon by the Republic. The wealthiest, able to provide themselves with a horse and the necessary equipment, served as cavalry, the

moderately well off as heavy infantry, the poorer as light infantry and the poorest rarely served at all. In a real sense the army represented a cross-section of Roman society under arms. For these men service in the army was not a career but a duty to the Republic. As men of property – most were farmers – they easily returned to civilian life after each period of service. However, as the empire expanded, wars tended to last longer and be fought further away, while there was a growing need for permanent garrisons to protect conquered territory. A decade of service in a garrison in one of the Spanish provinces could well mean ruination for the owner of a small farm. Service became increasingly unpopular and the eventual solution was to turn to men willing to make the army their profession. A soldier's pay was low, the conditions of his service extremely harsh, and a military career tended only to be attractive to the poorest citizens, who in the past had not been obliged

The Sacra Via ran through the heart of the Forum Romanum and was the route for a triumph. The Temple of the Divine Julius, visible on the left, was erected near the place where Caesar was cremated. (Author)

THE ROMAN WORLD IN 50 BC

REGNUM BOSPORI

Zela

PONTUS

CAPPADOCIA

Zeugma

Tarsus

Antioch

SYRIA

CILICIA

Xanthus

Tyre

Pelusium

GALATIA

BITHYNIA

Pergamum

Sardis

Ephesus

Alexandria

AEGYPTUS

Nilus

Philippi

Thessalonica

THESSALIA

Pharsalus

Athens

Corinth

Lissus

Dyrrhachium

Apollonia

EPIRUS

Patrae

Scodra

Oricum

Corcyra

Actium

ILLYRICUM

Ariminum

Brundisium

Perusia

Corfinium

Tarentum

Aquileia

Ravenna

Capua

Bononia

CISALPINE GAUL

ITALIA

Roma

Placentia

Po

SICILIA

Mutina

Lilybaeum

Utica

Hadrumetum

Leptis

CORSICA

SARDINIA

AFRICA

Ruspina

Thapsus

Bagradas

Massilia

NUMIDIA

Narbo

MAURETANIA

GALLIA

HISPANIA CITERIOR

Ilerda

Tarraco

Sicoris

Ebro

Corduba

Munda

HISPANIA ULTERIOR

Baetis

Hispalis

Gades

LUSITANI

Regions loyal to Pompey in late 50 BC

Regions loyal to Caesar in late 50 BC

0   100 miles

0   200 km

to serve. Such men proved excellent soldiers, but when the war ended and their legion was disbanded they had nothing to return to in civilian life. The Senate refused to acknowledge this change, maintaining that military service was a duty requiring no formal reward, and made no provision to provide for discharged soldiers. Individual commanders began to demand land for their veteran soldiers, wanting to settle them in colonies on conquered territory. Soldiers started to become more loyal to generals who offered such rewards than to the Republic which neglected them.

The rise of the professional army was probably the most important of the problems besetting the Republic with which the Senate failed to deal, but it was by no means the only one. Italy's economy and society had been profoundly changed by Roman expansion and the influx of huge numbers of slaves. The population of Rome itself had swollen to 1,000,000 by the end of the 1st century BC, a high proportion of them without steady employment. *Popularis* politicians who tried to address the problems of dispossessed farmers or the urban or rural poor were sure of winning support. All of these factors produced a dangerous instability. In 88 the consul Publius Cornelius Sulla led his legions to seize power in Rome when Marius tried to seize the command allocated to him. Civil war followed, leading to Sulla eventually becoming dictator for more than a year. After this, stability never really returned to the Republic for more than very brief periods, as attempted coups, political violence and civil war followed each other with monotonous regularity. Sulla was a member of an old aristocratic family that had fallen on hard times, and had to use extreme methods to achieve the distinguished position within the Republic that he felt his birth warranted. There were several other men from similar backgrounds who acted in a similar way, and the most successful of these was Caius Julius Caesar.

BACKGROUND TO WAR

The First Triumvirate

OPPOSITE

Pompey was
Caesar's ally in
59 BC; the bond
strengthened when
he married Caesar's
daughter. Her death,
and the death of
Crassus, weakened
the alliance and
contributed to the
Civil War. (Photo
by PHAS/Universal
Images Group via
Getty Images)

For nearly two years Sulla ruled as dictator with absolute power and only laid this down when he went into voluntary retirement. Before he did so, Sulla attempted to restore the Senate's position within the Republic, confirming its traditional powers and filling it with his supporters. He passed a law that was intended to prevent army commanders from following his own example and using their legions outside their own provinces without permission. The career pattern (*cursus honorum*) followed by Roman senators was also to be regulated more closely. The Republic was not to be dominated by a few individuals, but guided by the collective wisdom of the 600 senators.

Sulla's reforms were reactionary, impractical and weakened by the example of his own rise to power, so that many Romans did not consider them to be legitimate. Most importantly Sulla had failed to do anything to cater for the demands of the army on a permanent basis, so that discharged soldiers continued to have no source of livelihood and were therefore still inclined to follow any commander who promised them land. The chaos of the civil war and the rapid collapse of the Sullan constitution fostered a continuation of political disorder and eventually the renewal of open war in 49. This period also had a profound influence

on the careers and attitudes of the main protagonists in 49–45. Caesar himself first rose to prominence during Sulla's dictatorship, narrowly avoiding execution by the dictator when he publicly celebrated his relation by marriage to Marius at a family funeral.

However, a far more dramatic role was played by Cnaeus Pompey, who in 83 came to the support of Sulla at the head of three legions raised from his family's estates and veterans who had served under his late father, Pompeius Strabo ('squinty'). At the time Pompey was only 23 and, having never held public office, had no legal authority on which to base his power. Fighting with distinction in Italy, Sicily and north Africa, Pompey was granted the title Magnus ('The Great') by Sulla, though this may have been more than a little ironic. After Sulla's retirement, the Senate continued to employ the services of this private citizen and his personal army to suppress an attempted coup in Italy in 78 and then to fight the last of Marius' adherents in Spain. Employing Pompey, rather than a legally appointed magistrate under their control, set an exceptionally bad precedent. Probably the Senate felt that, since Pompey and his legions existed, it was better to use him than risk his turning against them.

In 71 Pompey returned victorious from Spain, and decided to stand for the consulship for the following year. He was too young, and had held none of the normally required junior magistracies, but he kept his legions outside the city as a scarcely veiled threat. Marcus Licinius Crassus, who had just returned from suppressing Spartacus's slave rebellion, took the opportunity to retain his own army and in turn declared himself a candidate for the consulship. Crassus was exceptionally wealthy, his fortune based originally on property confiscated from Sulla's executed opponents. The Senate was forced to permit their candidature and the Roman people, who were on the whole well disposed to both men after their successes, duly elected Pompey and Crassus as consuls for 70. Thus Pompey at the age of 36 entered the Senate directly as a consul, an utterly unprecedented action. His military record was already spectacular, but, given his age, he clearly expected to be given further important tasks.

Since Sulla's reforms, a magistrate remained in Rome itself during his year of office. He was then appointed as a promagistrate to govern a province. Former consuls, or proconsuls, were sent to the most important provinces while former praetors, or propraetors, went to the less significant areas. The appointment as governor was normally made for a year, but could, if the Senate chose, be renewed for additional 12-month periods at the end of this time. As governor, the promagistrate possessed supreme military and civil power within his province, dispensing legal decisions or leading an army as the situation required. He could not be recalled or prosecuted until his term of office expired. A governor's powers (or *imperium*) lapsed as soon as he re-entered Rome and he became a private citizen again, simply one senator among many. The Senate had traditionally chosen the provinces for each new political year, although individual magistrates were then normally allocated a task by lot. In 88 Marius had arranged for a popular vote giving him the command in the Asian War, a move which prompted Sulla's march on Rome. In 67 Pompey employed the same method of a vote in the People's Assembly (*concilium plebis*) to give him a wide-ranging command against the pirates plaguing the Mediterranean. A combination of careful organisation, massive resources, and a willingness to accept the surrender of pirate communities and resettle them elsewhere, allowed Pompey to achieve victory in under two months. In 66 another law was passed by the people sending Pompey to Asia to fight against Mithridates of Pontus. This meant that the existing commander in this war, Lucullus, who had achieved great success, was replaced in spite of the Senate's desire to leave him in charge. Since the war was virtually over before he arrived, it took little time for Pompey to complete the defeat of Mithridates, who committed suicide when his

own son turned against him. Pompey then proceeded to campaign throughout the near east, for instance, intervening in a domestic squabble between the kings of Judaea. After a three-month siege, Pompey took Jerusalem. He and his officers went into the Holy of Holies in the Great Temple, although they declined to take any of its treasures. This was a great propaganda success, the Roman aristocracy always striving to be the first to do any spectacular deed. As well as his military operations, Pompey carried out extensive administrative reform of the east. Provincial boundaries were altered, cities founded or refounded with new constitutions and relations with client kingdoms regulated. Many aspects of his settlement would endure for over 500 years.

Pompey had acquired so much glory and plunder on his campaigns that he had no serious rival within the Senate, and there was growing fear of what he would do when he returned to Italy. Many wondered whether he might copy Sulla and seize absolute power by force. In fact, Pompey behaved in a manner that was scrupulously correct, disbanding his army almost as soon as it had landed in Brundisium, and returning to Rome to celebrate an especially lavish triumph. He seems to have simply wanted to take his place as one of the Senate's most important members, but he also had two immediate political objectives. The first was to gain formal approval for all of his reforms in the eastern provinces. The second was to secure grants of land for the soldiers who had served him so well. In spite of his tremendous prestige, and in part because he had spent so much time on campaign and so little at Rome, Pompey was a poor politician. His speech in the Senate fell flat, and he did not seem to know how to use his great reputation and wealth to achieve his ends. He was opposed, most notably by Crassus, who was jealous of Pompey's prestige; Lucullus, who resented having been superseded in the command against Mithridates; and Cato the Younger, who disliked the revolutionary nature of Pompey's career and was reluctant to see him prosper. Time and again this opposition thwarted any attempt to ratify Pompey's settlement or grant land to his veterans.

OPPOSITE
Sulla was the first Roman to lead his legions against Rome itself. As dictator he ruthlessly slaughtered his enemies. Caesar's clemency was a deliberate attempt to show that he was different. (Photo by CM Dixon/Print Collector/Getty Images)

Roman public life was focused around the Forum in the heart of the city. As *pontifex maximus*, Caesar lived in the official residence or Regia on the right. (Author)

The impasse dragged on for nearly two years and was finally resolved in a manner that astounded most senators.

In 60 Julius Caesar returned from Further Spain, where he had served as a propraetorian governor and campaigned with success against local tribes. Six years younger than Pompey, Caesar's career had been fairly conventional up to this point, although his lavish spending on games and public feasting, combined with his rakish lifestyle, had won him numerous political enemies. Having won the right to celebrate a triumph, Caesar hoped this honour would permit him to win the consulship for 59. However, candidates had to present themselves for election in the city itself, and a general, still in command of the troops who would march in procession behind his chariot during the triumph, was not permitted to enter Rome until the day of the ceremony. Unable to gain an exemption, Caesar gave up his right to a triumph, dismissed his troops, and entered the city as a civilian. Thwarted, his opponents arranged for one of the consular provinces for the next year to be the supervision of the forests and country paths of Italy, a command without any troops or opportunities for profit and glory.

Around this time Caesar made approaches to both Crassus and Pompey and managed to reconcile them. Together the three men formed a secret political alliance, which is known by historians as the First Triumvirate. To cement the alliance, Pompey married Caesar's daughter Julia, a union which, for all its political inspiration, proved to be a remarkably happy one. In return for supporting his candidature, Caesar undertook to gain land for Pompey's veterans and to secure the ratification of his Eastern Settlement. Crassus paid off the massive debts Caesar had incurred in the promotion of his career, and gained a secure place as one of the most powerful men in the state. Caesar won the election and during his year of office was able to override his consular colleague, Lucius Calpurnius Bibulus. On several occasions large numbers of Pompey's veterans packed into the forum and voting assemblies, using threats or actual force to control the voting. One common joke at the time was that this year Rome had two consuls – Julius and Caesar. Together the three members of the triumvirate possessed massive patronage. Many senators owed them money, especially Crassus, who was highly skilled in using his fortune to win influence, and all had to go to the triumvirs if they wished to secure an appointment to any of the more senior positions in the army or government. Both Crassus and Pompey were highly satisfied and, in return, Caesar was granted a far more important province by popular vote. A special command consisting of three normal provinces, Illyricum, Cisalpine Gaul and Transalpine Gaul (modern-day Provence in southern France), was allocated to him for five years.

Caesar departed for his province in 58, never to return to Italy until the beginning of the Civil War. Crassus had covered his immediate debts, but Caesar was in great need of money to further his career. Very much the junior partner in the triumvirate, he also needed military glory to rival Crassus and, especially, Pompey. At first he appears to have contemplated a Balkan war against the Dacian King Burebista, but the news of the migration of a Gallic tribe towards Transalpine Gaul shifted his focus away from Illyricum. Over the next years Caesar campaigned throughout Gaul, twice bridged the Rhine and marched into Germany, and led two expeditions across the sea to Britain. That island remained mysterious to the Romans, and the euphoria over Caesar's expeditions could be compared to the excitement that greeted the moon landing in 1969. Caesar won massive glory during his Gallic campaigns, and produced his *Commentaries*, probably published in annual instalments, to celebrate his achievements. As well as gaining glory, Caesar became one of the wealthiest men in the world from plunder and sale of slaves, hundreds of thousands of whom were captured during the conflict.

Though unable to leave his province without also laying down his command, Caesar took care to keep a close eye on affairs in Rome, and spent every winter as close as possible, overseeing the administration of Cisalpine Gaul. He supported a radical politician, Publius Clodius, a demagogue who employed a gang of political thugs to force his legislation through. Rome had no police force, nor was it permitted for troops to be stationed within the city, so the state had no force with which to combat this violence. Clodius passed laws that complemented the legislation of Caesar's consulship, but which also attacked prominent figures within the Senate. In 58 Marcus Tullius Cicero was forced into exile, a success Clodius celebrated by leading a riot which burned down his house. Next Clodius turned his attention to Pompey, a move that presumably was not sanctioned by Caesar. Pompey responded by backing another gang of thugs led by Titus Annius Milo. Running battles were fought in and around Rome as

OPPOSITE
Caesar went to Gaul heavily in debt. From the plunder and the enslavement of around a million people, he returned as one of the richest men in the Roman world. (Photo By DEA PICTURE LIBRARY/De Agostini via Getty Images)

the city descended into chaos. In 57 Pompey sponsored a law recalling Cicero. Three days after Cicero's return, that is on 7 September, Pompey was given the major responsibility of overseeing the city's corn supply and once again displayed his considerable talents for organisation in rapidly remedying the situation. His return to the public eye provoked a renewal of rivalry with Crassus and it was clear that the triumvirate was coming under strain.

Crassus went to consult Caesar in his province and, after some cajoling, Pompey travelled to join them in April 56. In the town of Luca the triumvirs, along with a hundred or so senators who had accompanied them to show their goodwill, held a conference in which the alliance was patched up. Pompey and Crassus would both stand for the consulship in 55 and, since both their fame and the presence of a considerable body of Caesar's soldiers on leave ensured success, they were able to arrange matters to the benefit of all three. Caesar's command was extended for five years, although there is some doubt as to precisely when in late 50 or early 49 it was to expire. Pompey received both the Spanish provinces, but in an unprecedented move was allowed to remain in Rome and command through subordinates. Crassus was given Syria, from which he planned to lead an invasion of Parthia, for it seems that he felt the need to rival the conquests of his colleagues. Aged almost 60, he was considered rather old for active command by Roman standards and there were doubts about the legitimacy of a war with Parthia, but the triumvirs were too strong for any opposition to stand much chance.

In 54 Julia died in childbirth, and Crassus left to join the army in Syria. The following year he was defeated by the Parthians at Carrhae, and then killed when his army was forced to retreat. In spite of these blows, Pompey appeared still to consider himself bound to Caesar and in 53 sent one of his Spanish legions to reinforce Caesar's army in Gaul. Rome continued to be plagued by political violence, as Clodius' and Milo's followers clashed with renewed frenzy. In 52 Clodius was killed and his supporters carried his body into the Senate House, where they cremated it, burning the building to the ground in the process. In the face of anarchy, the Senate appointed Pompey sole consul and charged him with restoring order, for the first time permitting troops to guard Rome itself. Milo was put on trial and forced into exile as order was restored.

Caesar knew that he had many opponents in the Senate, chief among them Cato the Younger. In spite of his new wealth and the freedom with which he had tried to buy support, Caesar knew that a good number of influential men loathed him, and would not forgive him for his actions in 59. As a serving magistrate he was not subject to prosecution, but as soon as his office expired and he returned to civilian life this protection was withdrawn. He did not believe that he would receive a fair trial. During the Gallic campaigns Cato had even once suggested that he ought to be handed over to the Germans for war crimes. Defeat would mean exile and the end of his political career. To avoid this, Caesar wanted to go straight into a second consulship, after which he would be given another military command, perhaps against the Parthians. In this way he could continue to serve the Republic in a distinguished capacity.

In 52 Pompey passed a law which stipulated a five-year interval between a magistracy and a provincial command, although he specifically exempted Caesar in a clause apparently written in his own handwriting. However, around the same time he married the daughter of Publius Metellus Scipio, a known opponent of Caesar. Pressure on Caesar mounted, as incoming consuls lobbied to have him replaced in his province, since the war in Gaul appeared to be over. Pompey's attitude appeared increasingly ambivalent and the extension of his Spanish command gave him military might to match against Caesar. The latter was being forced into a corner. He had either to give up his command and trust to Pompey to protect him from the inevitable prosecution or to fight.

The death of Crassus after his defeat by the Parthians at Carrhae unbalanced the alliance with Pompey. Horse archers like this fought in a fundamentally different way to the legionaries. (Photo by CM Dixon/Print Collector/Getty Images)

WARRING SIDES

Legion against legion

Rome's civil wars split the state into factions, and the army with it. Since there were no ethnic, ideological or social differences between the rival sides, it was inevitable – even more than in any other civil war – that the organisation, tactical doctrine and equipment of their armies was virtually identical. The main strength of the Roman army lay in the legions, units with a paper strength of about 5,000. In theory the legions were recruited only from Roman citizens, but during the civil wars many non-citizens were enlisted to bolster numbers. In his *Commentaries*, Caesar frequently emphasised the heterogeneous nature of the enemy armies, but he had himself formed an entire legion, Legio V Alaudae, from Gauls, only later giving them the franchise as a reward for distinguished service. Given the dominance of the Roman military system, some allied kings had remodelled their armies after the Roman style. King Juba of Numidia included four legions in his large army, while Deiotarus of Galatia formed two which would later be amalgamated and formed into Legio XXII Deiotariana as a fully fledged part of the Roman army.

In this period a legion consisted entirely of heavy infantry. It had no permanent commander, but the practice had evolved of appointing an officer, usually one of the general's representatives, or legates, to fulfil this role. Much of the unit's administration was overseen by the six military tribunes, probably assisted by a small staff. These were largely equestrians (the class immediately below the Senate and possessing similar property) and at that time many were career soldiers of considerable experience. The basic tactical unit of the legion was the cohort of some 480 men. There were ten of these in each legion, and the cohort in turn was subdivided into six centuries of 80. The century was led by a centurion, supported by an *optio* (second-in-command), *signifer* (standard-bearer), and *tesserarius* (guard commander). Centurion represented a grade of officer rather than a specific rank and these men differed greatly in seniority. On several occasions Caesar mentions rewarding brave centurions by promoting them to a higher grade, often in a newly formed legion that would benefit from having experienced officers. One of the six centurions probably acted as commander of the cohort, either the man with longest service or the centurion of the senior century, the *pilus prior*.

This 1st century AD relief from the legionary base at Mainz depicts a legionary with a rectangular shield. Shields of this shape were common under the Principate and may already have been in use. (Photo © M.C. Bishop)

All legionaries were equipped with the same basic defensive gear, consisting of a bronze helmet (most often of Montefortino or Coolus patterns), cuirass (usually mail but sometimes of scale), and a large semi-cylindrical bodyshield constructed from three layers of plywood to give it both flexibility and strength. The latter seem most often to have been oval in shape, but it is possible that the transition to a more rectangular shape was already underway. Such shields were heavy – reconstructed examples have weighed in at 22lbs – but offered good protection. They could also be used offensively, the soldier punching forward with all his body weight behind the shield's bronze boss. We are told that one of Caesar's soldiers, in spite of having his right hand chopped off almost as soon as he had boarded a warship,

The Coolus-type helmet (the name is modern) was one of the commonest patterns worn by legionaries in the late Republic. Many were cheaply made. (© The Trustees of the British Museum)

was able to clear the deck of enemies by knocking them down with his shield during the fighting off Massila. A soldier's other offensive equipment consisted of a short sword, the famed *gladius*, sometimes a dagger, and a heavy throwing javelin known as the *pilum*. The *pilum* consisted of a wooden haft about 4 feet long, topped by a narrow iron shank 2 feet in length and ending in a pyramid-shaped point. When thrown, all of its great weight was concentrated behind this small tip, giving it formidable penetrative power. It was designed so that once it punched through an enemy's shield, the slim iron shank would slide easily through the hole made by the point and had the reach to wound the man behind. Soldiers may have carried two *pila* on campaign, but only one on the day of battle itself. The doctrine of the period was to deliver a massed volley at very short range

– some 15 yards or so – and follow this up with a charge, sword in hand.

Roman legionaries were not simply soldiers, for many were trained as engineers or artillerymen. Such men remained with their cohorts until required, and were then formed in temporary units to complete a task. The Civil War would be marked by many remarkable feats of engineering.

In battle a legion most often formed in three lines, four cohorts in the first line and three each in the second and third. Intervals were maintained between each unit and the cohorts from the next line stationed to cover these gaps, creating something resembling a checkerboard formation. However, since all cohorts were armed uniformly, the legion was perfectly capable of fighting effectively in other formations, and we also hear of armies in four or two lines, although a single line was considered too brittle to be employed save in dire need. The legion was a very flexible force. Its structure and size made it an important subunit within the battle line, but one or several cohorts could as easily be detached for smaller operations. As with all armies throughout history, theoretical unit sizes were rarely reflected in the field. At Pharsalus the cohorts of Pompey's legions averaged around 400 men apiece, while Caesar's force was little more than half that size. Campaign attrition reduced one of Caesar's legions to less than 1,000 men during the Egyptian campaign.

The legions were the mainstay of any army, especially decisive in pitched battles, but both sides supplemented their numbers with allied soldiers or auxiliaries, fighting in their own traditional style. Such troops were especially useful in providing cavalry and light infantry. In most cases they were locally recruited and led by their own native chieftains. At first Caesar's auxiliaries came primarily from the Gallic and German tribes, and

The Kasr el-Harit shield was found in Egypt and is almost certainly Roman. Made from three layers of plywood, it is remarkably similar to ancient descriptions of the standard legionary shield. (Photo © Raffaele D'Amato)

This iron helmet, of the pattern known today as the Agen type, was one of several Gallic designs copied by the Romans, as well as continuing in use with auxiliaries from Gaul. (Swiss National Museum, A-14037)

Pompey's from his provinces in Spain and his many clients in the east, but as the war progressed, troops were recruited wherever possible and the pattern became more complex.

By the end of the Gallic campaigns, Caesar commanded ten legions (numbered V to XIV). Two more, XV and I, the latter on loan from Pompey's Spanish armies, had been withdrawn earlier in 50 to be sent against the Parthians. The majority of these troops were seasoned veterans, utterly devoted to Caesar and confident in their own and their commander's ability. In support were bands of excellent Gallic and German cavalry. To match against this Pompey had seven legions garrisoning his Spanish provinces, although these had little actual combat experience. There were also the I and the XV which had not yet left for the east and were still in Italy, but as both had recently served under Caesar their loyalty appeared questionable. However, he boasted that he had only to stamp his foot in Italy for more legions to appear, and was also sure of the loyalty of the eastern provinces which he had reorganised just over a decade before. In the long term, Pompey could probably claim greater resources than Caesar, but it would take time to mobilise these into field armies.

In 49 Pompey was almost 58, but remained an extremely fit and active man, and others marvelled at the energy he showed in joining the training exercises of his soldiers. His military record was extremely good, even if he had made something of a habit of arriving in the last stages of a conflict to claim the credit largely won by someone else. He was certainly a brilliant organiser, as the campaign against the pirates, as well as, more recently, his supervision of Rome's corn supply, had shown. In his youth he had been a bold commander, on several occasions leading charges in person, but his aggression, in a properly Roman way, had always been based on sound preparation. However, although he was only six years older than Caesar, Pompey had spent the last decade in Rome and had not served on campaign since 62. His performance during the Civil War would suggest that he was past his best as a general. He was not helped by the presence of so many distinguished senators in his camp. Unlike Caesar, whose followers were undistinguished and whose authority was unchallenged, Pompey was always under pressure to alter his plans. Most of the senators who flocked to his cause had more prestige than ability, and on more than a few occasions proved a positive hindrance. The ablest of his subordinates, Titus Atius Labienus, had served with Caesar throughout the Gallic campaigns. It is probable that he had a prior connection with Pompey, for he defected from Caesar's camp at the beginning of the war. On hearing of this, the latter ordered his baggage to be sent on after him.

NEXT PAGES
The two legionaries on the Ahenobarbus monument may well give a good idea of the appearance of a soldier during the Civil War. Mail armour, oval shields and crested or plumed helmets appear to have been standard at this time. (Author)

Caesar failed to attract any distinguished supporters from the senior members of the Senate. Now in his early 50s, he was still very much at the peak of his ability, and was fresh from a decade of successful fighting in Gaul. His strategy during the Civil War, as in Gaul, was based on rapid offensives, sometimes in the face of great odds. Though often criticised for recklessness by modern commentators, it is important to emphasise that such boldness was characteristically Roman, and should not conceal that much preparation underlay these enterprises. Although subject to occasional epileptic fits, he was in other respects an extremely healthy and active man, capable of massive effort and rapid long-distance travel. Caesar promoted and lavishly rewarded any soldiers who distinguished themselves, but even more than this it was his remarkable charisma that ensured that his soldiers were devoted to him. Throughout the war, desertions from the Pompeian forces were common, but all of our sources claim that there were no defections in the other direction. Fighting a war to protect his own honour and status, Caesar's objective was clear and obvious, giving the Caesarian war effort a unity of purpose not displayed by the other side. Yet it also meant that it was much easier for him to lose. If Caesar were killed, or his army defeated so heavily that he was discredited, then the war would effectively have been over. Only the Pompeians could suffer defeat after defeat and still prolong the struggle.

It is hard now to say whether Pompey or Caesar was the better general. The vast bulk of our evidence comes, directly or indirectly, from Caesar's version of events. His *Commentaries* obviously present his own actions in a favourable light, while dismissing those of the enemy. However, they also provide evidence that allows the wisdom of some of Caesar's decisions to be questioned. Yet, for the Romans the answer was obvious, for the most important attribute of a great general was that he won his wars. Caesar defeated Pompey, and in the end there was no more to be said.

OUTBREAK

Crossing the Rubicon

'They wanted it. Were it not for the support of my army they would have passed judgement upon me in spite of my achievements.' (Caesar looking at the bodies of dead senators after Pharsalus)

By 50 the mood in Rome was increasingly tense. The fear was similar to that in anticipation of Pompey's return in 62, but probably even worse, for Caesar was perceived now as a more open revolutionary, and his province, with its large, veteran army, lay on Italy's own border. Many Romans feared that this force would be turned against the state in a bid for dictatorship. A much smaller group of senators, led by Cato and including many of the House's most influential members, was determined that Caesar should not be allowed to return to normal politics, since his new-found wealth and prestige would make it difficult to oppose him. Were he allowed a second consulship, it was feared that his behaviour this time would be even worse than in 59. Everyone realised that Pompey's attitude would be decisive, but his intentions remained unclear. Stopping Caesar from arranging to stand *in absentia* (and so retaining his army) for the consulship required at the very least Pompey's inaction, while if it came to a war, he was the only one capable of matching Caesar's military might. Yet if Caesar was defeated and killed or exiled,

this would remove Pompey's last serious rival, leaving him with massively greater power, influence and wealth than anyone else within the Republic. This in itself threatened monarchy, but Cato and his supporters clearly believed this to be the lesser of two evils. At worst Pompey was a less skilful politician than Caesar and so would have greater difficulty in exploiting his position, but it seems likely that they hoped in some way to negate him. Perhaps the only real chance for the Republic would have been to accept Caesar's return and continue to have two leading senators or *principes* far outstripping their fellows and so balancing each other's power. Even if this had occurred, there was always the risk that the two would fall out at a later date and that a war would result. In the event, intransigence on both sides prevented any compromise.

In 51 Caesar had tried to have his command extended until the very end of 49, presumably so that he could then move directly into the consulship for 48, but the measure was successfully opposed in the Senate, in part because Pompey failed to support it. This was followed by several attempts to have Caesar recalled immediately, using the argument that the war in Gaul had already been completed. Pompey opposed these moves, and in March 50 made it clear that Caesar ought to be permitted the original extent of his governorship, no more and no less. The failure to support his old ally more fully encouraged the belief that there was a split between the two.

In the meantime Caesar had been employing the profits of his campaigns to buy influence and friends at Rome. One of the consuls of 50, Lucius Aemilius Paullus, allegedly received 36,000,000 sesterces (as a guide an ordinary soldier was paid 1,000 sesterces a year), enough to cover the great debts he had incurred in restoring the Basilica Aemilia (originally built by an ancestor) in the forum. Paullus did not support his colleague Caius Claudius Marcellus in his attacks on Caesar. More active support was purchased from the tribune of the plebs Caius Scribonius Curio, at the cost of 10,000,000, which also went mainly to his many

OPPOSITE
Marcus Porcius Cato commanded immense respect, but less firm support. Uncle and a great inspiration to Brutus, his intransigence helped to make the Civil War inevitable. (Photo By DEA / G. DAGLI ORTI/De Agostini via Getty Images)

creditors. Curio was highly talented, but unreliable, having been involved with many of the scandals of the last decade, and had previously been vocal in his condemnation of Caesar. Now he proved vigorous in his support of Caesar's objectives throughout his year as tribune. In the Senate he argued that Pompey's Spanish command should end at the same time as Caesar's post, although it in fact had several years still to run. More than a few senators responded favourably to this idea, hoping that in this way open war between the two men could be averted. When the Senate finally voted on this proposal on 1 December 50, it was carried by 370 votes to 22. However, in the same session Marcellus arranged for them also to vote separately on whether Caesar and Pompey should be removed from their commands. A large majority was in favour of Caesar laying down his governorship, and as big a majority against forcing Pompey to do so. Rejecting the Senate's decision that both should give up their armies, Marcellus and a group of supporters went to call on Pompey. Giving him a sword, they requested that he take action to preserve the Republic. Pompey neither accepted nor declined this task, and the city's uncertainty deepened. Then, a few days later he seemed to have declared himself openly, and took command of two legions, I and XV. Veterans from his old armies were summoned to Rome.

Curio's term as tribune expired later in the month, but another of Caesar's supporters, Mark Antony, had been elected to the office and continued his work. In the meantime Caesar had written to the Senate, recounting his many victories won on Rome's behalf and his other services to the state, reminding them that he had already been granted the right to stand for consulship *in absentia*, and offering to lay down his command, provided that Pompey did the same thing. If he did not, then Caesar felt that he was obliged to retain his legions as protection against the faction opposed to him. The letter included the scarcely veiled threat that he was also willing to free Rome from the tyranny of this faction. On the same day that this was read in the Senate, Pompey's father-in-law,

OPPOSITE
Mark Antony came from a more distinguished family than most of Caesar's supporters, but shared their reputation for wild living and radical politics. His military experience was limited. (Photo By DEA / A. DAGLI ORTI/De Agostini via Getty Images)

Scipio, proposed issuing a decree that Caesar must hand over his legions by a set date – probably some time in the summer – but the measure was vetoed by the tribunes. Another group of senators, this time headed by Caesar's father-in-law, Calpurnius Piso, asked leave of absence to visit Caesar in his province and negotiate with him, but this was refused. Curio acted as Caesar's representative and proposed various compromises, at first that Caesar would give up the main military province, Transalpine Gaul, later extended to Cisalpine Gaul. He would remain governor of Illyricum with command of just one legion, but must be allowed to stand *in absentia* for the consulship. If the offer was serious, and we have no reason to doubt that it was, this would have made it virtually impossible for Caesar to fight a civil war and seize power by force. Pompey seems to have been tempted, but Cato and his associates so detested Caesar that they simply would not accept his standing for election without first becoming a private citizen, and therefore subject to prosecution. Another suggestion, supported by Cicero, was that at the same time Pompey should leave Italy and actually go to govern his Spanish provinces. One of the consuls for 49, Lucius Lentulus Cornelius Crus was violently opposed to any compromise, and continually insulted both Antony and Curio.

On 7 January 49 the Senate met and passed its ultimate decree, the *senatus consultum ultimum*, which called on the magistrates to use any means to defend the state. Caesar's supporters among the tribunes felt threatened with physical assault if they remained in the city. Disguised as slaves, they were hidden in carts and fled north to join Caesar, as did Curio. In the coming months Caesar's propaganda would exploit the threats made to the tribunes of the plebs, for this office was held in particular respect and affection by the population as a whole. In the days to come Pompey and the Senate began to prepare the war effort against Caesar. Scipio was given command of Syria, and Lucius Domitius Ahenobarbus, consul in 54 and a long-time opponent of Caesar, received the Gallic provinces.

The news reached Caesar at Ravenna on 10 January. He spent the day watching gladiators training and held a previously arranged dinner in the evening, but secretly issued orders for several parties of soldiers to travel in civilian clothes carrying concealed weapons to Ariminum (modern Rimini), the nearest town in Italy. With him he had only a single legion, XIII, and apparently some 300 cavalrymen. Late in the evening he excused himself to his guests, and then departed for Ariminum in a carriage drawn by two mules. One tradition claims that in the night they lost their way, and it was only after they had found a local guide that they returned to the right road and reached the river Rubicon, which marked the boundary of his province. Commanders were barred by law from leading troops outside their province without the Senate's express permission, so crossing the river would turn Caesar into a rebel. In some versions Caesar paused uncertainly for some time, discussing with his officers what he should do. One of these was Asinius Pollio, who later wrote a history of the war (now sadly lost), so it is possible that he was truly indecisive and that these accounts are not simply inventions intended to heighten dramatic tension. Less likely is the story that they were confronted by the vision of a god playing pipes. However long it took, Caesar crossed the Rubicon, uttering the famous line 'the die is cast' – *alea iacta est* in Latin, although some versions claim that he spoke in Greek.

Caesar and his men occupied Ariminum without a fight and were soon joined by the tribunes. There was widespread fear of what he would do next. Cicero's correspondence from the early weeks of 49 is filled with gloomy forecasts of the bloodshed which everyone was sure would accompany the advance of the Caesarian army. In Gaul, Caesar and his legions had fought very aggressively and often with extreme brutality; some sources claimed that over a million people had been killed in less than a decade. Perhaps, as some modern commentators claim, many expected the legions to behave in no less harsh a manner now that they had burst

Caesar often mentions summoning his officers to a *consilium* or meeting. Although debate did occur, this was essentially a chance for the commander to issue orders and inspire his senior leaders. (Author)

into Italy, and Cicero on one occasion even wondered whether Caesar would not prove more like Hannibal than a Roman general. Yet we should remember that nearly all Romans, including Cicero and many opponents, had revelled in Caesar's victories over foreign enemies. Cato had wanted to have Caesar prosecuted for breach of faith when he attacked during a truce, and was not primarily concerned with the massacre of barbarian tribesmen. Far more worrying to contemporaries was the precedent of every civil war and rebellion fought in the previous 40 years. Marius had massacred any opponents he could catch when he seized Rome in 87. Sulla had made the process more formal, with the proscriptions, long lists of names posted in the forum. Any citizen proscribed lost all his legal rights; this made it legitimate for anyone to kill him and in doing so they would gain a share of the victim's property that would otherwise go to the state. Rome's civil wars were not fought between rival political ideologies but rival individuals, and normally ended in the death of all those on the losing side. There was no reason to suspect that Caesar would be any different, and the political violence he had employed during his consulship only seemed to make this more likely.

In fact the war did not begin as anyone had expected. Caesar moved quickly, seizing towns with the limited forces at his disposal rather than waiting to gather his legions. He was largely unopposed, but the advance of his army was not accompanied by massacre or atrocity and his soldiers were under strict orders not to loot. There was a strange, phoney-war quality to the first few weeks. Caesar in particular, was trying to show that he was still willing to compromise. Messages went back and forth as he suggested various compromises. Pompey and his allies replied by saying that they could not negotiate while Caesar commanded troops on Italian soil, and that he must return to Cisalpine Gaul before anything could be discussed. Yet Pompey did offer to leave for Spain once Caesar had laid down his command. Caesar refused the offer, perhaps not trusting the Senate or maybe feeling that he had gone too far to withdraw at this stage.

OPPOSITE
An early 2nd century AD monument from Romania depicts a legionary slashing with his gladius. Army training was based on gladiatorial training and taught both thrusts and cuts. (Author)

Even so, both sides continued to claim publicly that they still hoped for a negotiated settlement, and were only thwarted by the enemy's intransigence.

THE FIGHTING

Civil War

'Blitzkrieg' – The Italian campaign – January–March 49

The suddenness of Caesar's advance surprised and unnerved his opponents, just as he had intended. Pompey left Rome in the second half of January, declaring that it could not be defended. He was followed by most of the magistrates, including the consuls, who left in such haste that it suggested panic. Many Romans were still uncertain about just how firmly committed each side was to fighting, and this open admission of military weakness made many wonder whether Pompey could really be relied on to defend the Republic.

The first clash came at Corfinum, where Domitius Ahenobarbus had mustered some 30 cohorts of new recruits and planned to hold the city. This was in spite of Pompey's repeated pleas for Domitius to bring his men south to join his two legions (I and XV) at Capua. It was the first sign of the great divisions between the commanders opposing Caesar. Caesar's army now mustered two legions, for he had been joined by the XII, plus some Gallic cavalry, although some detachments from these units were probably still scattered as garrisons in the towns already occupied. In February Corfinum was surrounded and Ahenobarbus learned that Pompey had no intention of coming to his aid. Caesar tells us

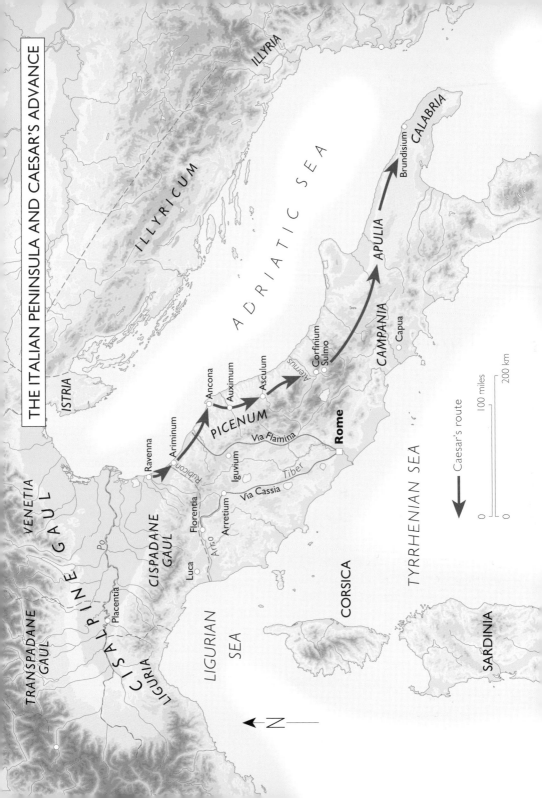

THE ITALIAN PENINSULA AND CAESAR'S ADVANCE

ILLYRIA

ILLYRICUM

ISTRIA

VENETIA GAUL

TRANSPADANE GAUL

CISALPINE GAUL

CISPADANE GAUL

LIGURIA

Po

Placentia

Luca

Florentia

Arno

Arretium

Via Cassia

Iguvium

Via Flamina

Tiber

Ravenna

Ariminum

Rubicon

PICENUM

Ancona

Auximum

Asculum

Aternus

Corfinium

Sulmo

Deira

Capua

CAMPANIA

APULIA

Brundisium

CALABRIA

Rome

ADRIATIC SEA

LIGURIAN SEA

TYRRHENIAN SEA

CORSICA

SARDINIA

N

Caesar's route

100 miles

200 km

0

0

EXTESTAM
P·GESSI·P·L
PRIMI

GESSIA·P·L·FAVSTA·P·GESS

that Ahenobarbus then panicked and planned to slip out of the city and escape, abandoning his soldiers to their fate. Hearing of this, the garrison mutinied and surrendered themselves and the town. Ahenobarbus and the other senators were brought before Caesar, who made a great display of formally telling them of the grievances that had prompted him to march into Italy, and then allowing all who wished to, to go free. This was the first important display of Caesar's clemency (*clementia*), a policy to which he would adhere throughout the conflict, in marked contrast to his opponents, who employed the more brutal methods normal in past civil wars. The ordinary soldiers and most of their officers took an oath of allegiance to Caesar and were taken into his own army.

Pompey had probably already decided to abandon Italy altogether and cross the Adriatic to Greece. In the eastern provinces he had many clients and allies who could provide him with soldiers. The only properly trained troops in Italy had until recently been serving

SP FRONIA P GESSIVS P LBER IVANS

A RBIT
GESSIA
FAVSTA

under Caesar, and Pompey was reluctant to test their loyalty so soon by advancing on the enemy. With Domitius's army gone, he was in any case outnumbered. He would go east, recruit and train a vast army and fleet and deal with Caesar in due course, returning to invade Italy by sea. Often he is supposed to have declared that 'Sulla did it, why shouldn't I?', referring to the dictator's successful return from the east in 83. Militarily this plan made perfect sense, but politically it was very damaging. Many Romans felt abandoned, and one senator sarcastically reminded Pompey that if he was short of soldiers to fight Caesar then perhaps he ought to start stamping his feet.

Pompey retreated south to Brundisium. Caesar followed in pursuit as quickly as he could, but a large number of recruits and senators had already been shipped across the Adriatic before he arrived outside the city. Pompey remained with about two legions, waiting for the ships to return and complete the evacuation. Caesar's engineers began to supervise the construction

The tombstone of Publius Gessius depicts him in cuirass and with a sword, which presumably means that he was an officer around the time of the Civil War. The men on either side are his freedmen. (Photograph © 2022 Museum of Fine Arts, Boston. All rights reserved. / Archibald Cary Coolidge Fund / Bridgeman Images)

Roman legionaries acted as engineers and labourers as well as infantry. Both sides in the Civil War made roads and fortified lines with great skill and speed. (Author)

of a huge mole, intended to block access to the harbour. At first a solid breakwater was built out from the shore, but in deeper water this was continually swept away, so instead they began adding large rafts to the structure. Pompey used merchant vessels mounting hastily constructed three-storey towers and equipped with light artillery to attack and hinder construction. Pompey's fleet returned before the mole was complete and were able to enter the harbour and embark the garrison. The city's gates were blocked and a small force left as rearguard to allow a smooth evacuation, but the citizens of Brundisium, either through hostility towards Pompey or fear of Caesar's men, helped the attackers in and the retreat became more hasty than planned.

In less than two months Caesar had seized control in Italy. Pompey had escaped, with the best of his soldiers, and many leading senators. At present Caesar lacked a fleet and was in no position to follow him. On 18 March he was back in Rome, trying to persuade as many senators as possible to convene. His clemency had surprised and relieved many who were neutral or wavering, though some were still convinced that this was simply a ploy and that, in time, Caesar's own cruel nature or that of his disreputable followers would prevail. When he led his soldiers to seize the state Treasury held in the Temple of Saturn, and Caesar threatened to execute the tribune Metellus who stood in his way, such fears seemed confirmed.

Curio was sent with two legions to secure Sardinia and then Africa. Caesar himself decided to set out for Spain overland and defeat Pompey's legions there. These were the best of the enemy troops then in existence, but their strategic role was unclear now that Pompey had shifted his main focus to the eastern Mediterranean. Caesar is supposed to have claimed that he went first to fight an army without a leader, before going to fight a leader without an army.

'An army without a leader' – the Spanish campaign – April–August 49

The main Pompeian army in Spain was at Ilerda (modern Lérida) and was commanded by Lucius Afranius and Marcus Petreius. Between them they had five legions, 80 cohorts of Spanish auxiliaries – a mixture of both close- and open-order infantry – and 5,000 cavalry. The other two legions, again supported by auxiliaries, remained far to the west in Further Spain under the command of Marcus Terentius Varro. To face the force at Ilerda, Caesar was able to muster six legions, along with 3,000 cavalry of various nationalities which had served with his army throughout the Gallic campaigns, and the same number of recently recruited Gauls. Also mentioned is a force of 900 horsemen kept as his personal bodyguard, but it is not entirely clear whether these were included in the above total. Most of

this force was sent on in advance under the command of Caius Fabius. As Caesar marched to join them, his tribunes and centurions offered to loan him money with which to pay the soldiers. Gratefully accepting this gesture, their commander felt that this commitment helped bond both officers and legionaries to his cause.

Ilerda lies on a ridge to the west of the river Sicoris (modern Segre). A small force covered the bridge outside the town, but the main Pompeian camp was situated further south on the same high ground, where they had gathered considerable store of provisions from the surrounding area. On arrival Fabius built two bridges across the river and crossed to camp on the west bank. Finding it difficult to gather food and fodder, he sent a foraging expedition of two legions back across to the eastern side, but this was threatened when one of the bridges unexpectedly collapsed and only rescued when a force was sent to its aid.

Caesar arrived in June, and immediately advanced and offered battle at the foot of the ridge. When Afranius refused to be drawn, Caesar had the third of his three lines dig a deep trench – a rampart would have been more visible and would therefore have invited attack – and then camped behind it. It took several days to complete the defences of this camp to Caesar's satisfaction, and after that he attempted to seize the hill between Ilerda and the enemy camp. Three legions formed for battle, and then the front line of one advanced to capture the height. The Pompeians responded quickly, and, moving swiftly and operating in a looser order learned in fighting the tribes of Lusitania (roughly the area of modern-day Portugal), occupied and defended the hilltop. Both sides fed in reinforcements throughout the day, although the narrow slope only allowed three cohorts in the fighting line at any one time. In the end, Legio IX charged uphill and drove the enemy back for sufficient time to permit Caesar's army to withdraw. They had lost 70 dead, including the senior centurion (*primus pilus*) of Legio XIV, and over 600 wounded, while the enemy had suffered 200 fatalities including five centurions.

OPPOSITE
An Iberian warrior in traditional dress wielding a curved sword or falcata. Spanish troops played a major role in the Civil War, but it is unclear whether they used traditional or Roman equipment. (Photo by: Universal History Archive/ Universal Images Group via Getty Images)

This coin was minted by Quintus Cassius Longinus, one of Caesar's supporters who provoked his own troops to mutiny. He was a cousin of Caius Cassius the conspirator, illustrating the splits within the senatorial class. (Johny SYSEL, CC BY-SA 3.0)

Two days later heavy rainfall raised the level and power of the river and swept away the bridges used by Caesar's army, largely cutting them off from supplies. Coming under increasing pressure, Caesar's soldiers built boats of the type they had seen in Britain. Ferrying a legion across the Sicoris at night, they secured a bridgehead and permitted the construction of a new bridge, allowing the army once again to operate effectively on the eastern bank as well as the west, winning several small engagements. This success encouraged many local communities to join Caesar, providing new sources of food. His engineers then dug canals off from the main river, lowering its level and creating a serviceable ford for men on horseback much nearer to the army's camp than the bridge. More Gallic cavalry had arrived, giving Caesar's horsemen a considerable numerical advantage over the Pompeians which soon made it increasingly difficult for their foraging parties to operate.

Afranius and Petreius decided that they could no longer maintain their position and so, using barges gathered from along the river as pontoons, they threw another bridge across the Sicoris and under cover of darkness crossed to the east bank, before turning south. Caesar's scouts reported this activity and in response he sent his cavalry to harass the enemy retreat, the rest of the army following at dawn. His men waded through the rudimentary ford, the infantry moving between two lines of pack animals to slow the flow of water. In the next days, Caesar's patrols discovered a more direct path than the enemy and by hard marching he was able to get in front of them. The enemy were now at a severe disadvantage, but Caesar refused the pleas of his officers and men to fight a battle,

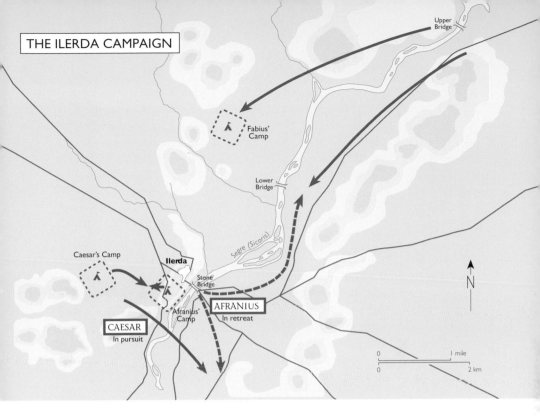

Fabius'
Camp

Upper
Bridge

Lower
Bridge

Segre (Sicoris)

Caesar's Camp

Ilerda

Stone
Bridge

Afranius'
Camp

AFRANIUS
In retreat

CAESAR
In pursuit

N

0   1 mile
0   2 km

saying that he hoped to win with as little loss of Roman life as possible. Camped close together, the legionaries on both sides began to fraternise. Nervous of their men's loyalty, Afranius and Petreius massacred all of Caesar's men they could catch, though their opponent released all the Pompeian soldiers in his camp unharmed. They then made their officers and men swear an oath not to abandon the cause. In spite of this, within a short time, the generals, their troops cut off from all supplies, capitulated. The commanders were pardoned and allowed to go free, some of the army incorporated into Caesar's own and the rest disbanded. Varro and the two legions in Further Spain surrendered immediately on the approach of Caesar's forces. In a matter of months, and through a mixture of boldness and skilful manoeuvre, Caesar had overrun Spain at minimal loss to himself. Appointing Quintus Cassius Longinus as governor – an extraordinary appointment for a man serving as tribune of the plebs – he returned to Italy.

Massilia – spring–summer 49

En route to Spain, Caesar had been refused admission to the great trading city of Massilia (modern Marseilles) by the authorities there, who claimed that they wished to remain neutral. The claim was immediately discredited when Domitius Ahenobarbus sailed into the harbour and took command of the city. Leaving Caius Trebonius with three legions and Decimus Brutus with a fleet to prosecute the siege, he had then moved on to Spain. The defenders proved very active, displaying especial skill in the small but fierce naval actions fought outside the harbour. Yet the attackers persisted in spite of heavy damage inflicted on their siege works by enemy sorties, and in the end the Massiliotes decided to surrender. Ahenobarbus learned of this, and fled by sea. Caesar, returning from Spain in late September, was present to accept the surrender, installing a garrison of two legions, but generally being lenient to the city.

Curio in Africa – spring–summer 49

Curio occupied Sicily without fighting, and then crossed with three legions to Africa, where the governor, Publius Attius Varus, had declared against Caesar. Varus was supported by the Numidian King Juba, who commanded a large, if sometimes unreliable army. Curio had little military experience – none at all of high command – and was considered brilliant but unreliable by most contemporaries. His army consisted of troops originally raised by the Pompeians who had taken the oath to Caesar after their surrender at Corfinum. Curio landed successfully near Utica, surprising the enemy, and soon came into contact with Varus' army. The two sides formed for battle on either side of a steep valley. Varus' brother, Sextus, had been at Corfinum and appealed to Curio's legions to desert and return to their original loyalty. However, the soldiers refused and, after a success in a cavalry skirmish, Curio led them in a bold, uphill attack which swiftly routed Varus' army. Encouraged by this success, Curio acted on what proved

to be faulty intelligence, and attacked what he believed was a detachment of Juba's army. In fact, the bulk of the king's forces was there and, after an initial success, the Romans were ambushed and virtually annihilated. Curio was surrounded with the remnants of his troops on a hilltop and died fighting. Only a small fraction of the army, including the historian Asinius Pollio, escaped to Sicily.

This early 1st century AD relief on the Arch of Orange shows how difficult it was for artists to depict the chaos of battle. (Patrick, Flickr, CC BY-SA 2.0)

'A leader without an army' – Greece – January–August 48

The report of Curio's defeat was not the only bad news reaching Caesar in late 49, for Mark Antony had suffered a lesser defeat in Illyricum. Even more serious was a mutiny involving four of his legions, and in particular Legio IX, at Placentia (modern Piacenza) on the river Po. The troops complained that many who had served throughout the Gallic campaigns were now long overdue for discharge, and that no one had yet received the donative of 500 denarii per man (double their annual salary) promised by Caesar at Brundisium some months before. Caesar's response was harsh, berating them for their impatience and declaring that he would decimate Legio IX, which meant executing one man in ten. In the end he relented, and only had the 12 ringleaders killed.

Dyrrachium

Caesar spent a short time at Rome, having been appointed dictator before he arrived and held the post for 11 days, using his powers to hold elections in which he was voted to the consulship. He was eager to move against Pompey, and near the end of the year went to join the army of some 12 legions along with 1,000 cavalry which had been assembled at Brundisium. Attrition meant that it was unlikely any of the legions mustered more than 3,000 men, and some units were closer to the 2,000 mark. Nevertheless, this was still a formidable total to ship across the Adriatic and to supply once there. Caesar exhorted his soldiers by saying that this next campaign would be the culmination of their labours, and then told them to carry only the absolutely essential baggage and to leave nearly all servants, slaves and families behind. On 4 January 48, there were sufficient ships to embark seven legions and 500 cavalrymen. The crossing was a great gamble, for Caesar had no significant naval force with which to oppose the vast Pompeian fleet, currently commanded by his old enemy and consular colleague in 59, Bibulus. Yet the enemy did not expect him to move in winter when the weather was poor, and Caesar landed without opposition at Paeleste in Epirus. Bibulus was alerted by the time the transport ships headed back to Brundisium and intercepted some of them. For the moment it proved impossible for Mark Antony to run the blockade and bring the remainder of the army across to join Caesar.

Caesar was isolated and severely outnumbered by the enemy. Pompey had had more than nine months to muster his forces, and by this time they amounted to nine legions, supported by over 5,000 light infantry and 7,000 cavalry. A further two legions under Scipio were on their way from Syria. Pompey, always a great organiser, had taken care to gather plenty of food and fodder to supply his troops even in the winter months. Caesar's men had to make do with the little they had brought with them and whatever could be gathered from local communities. The situation was increasingly desperate, but Caesar was not really strong enough to open a full-scale offensive. Some manoeuvring took place, along with further attempts at negotiation, but there was no serious fighting. At one point he put to sea in a small ship during appalling weather, hoping to reach Brundisium and hurry his reinforcements over, but the weather proved so bad that he was forced to return to the shore. In was not until 10 April that Mark Antony managed to bring the remaining legions across the Adriatic. Pompey responded too slowly and failed to prevent the union of the two forces.

Caesar had all 11 legions, but was still outnumbered and continued to have supply problems. Nevertheless he immediately resolved to make a bold attack on one of the enemy's major supply dumps at the port city of Dyrrachium. Outmarching the enemy, he managed to get between Pompey and the city, although he was not able to seize the latter. Pompey camped on the coast on a hill called Petra, overlooking a natural harbour which continued to allow him to receive supply shipments.

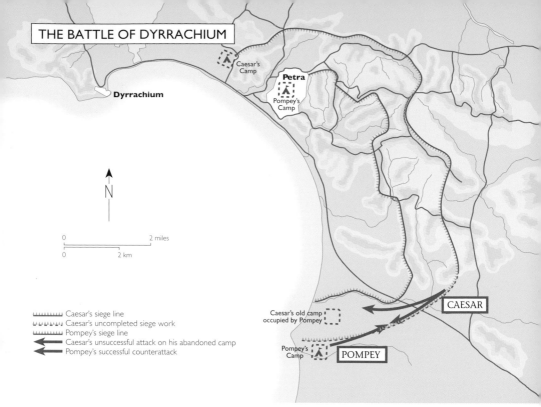

Caesar's
Camp

Petra

Pompey's
Camp

Dyrrachium

N

0   2 miles

0   2 km

Caesar's siege line
Caesar's uncompleted siege work
Pompey's siege line
Caesar's unsuccessful attack on his abandoned camp
Pompey's successful counterattack

Caesar's old camp
occupied by Pompey

CAESAR

Pompey's
Camp

POMPEY

Caesar's main camp was on a hill further north, but he
continued to have supply problems as the harvest was not
yet ripe and the region had been thoroughly plundered by
the enemy. A line of hills ran around Pompey's camp and
Caesar began construction of a line of forts connected
by a ditch and wall, which were intended eventually to
surround the enemy completely. This provided some
protection for his patrols and foraging parties from the
more numerous enemy cavalry, although in part the
rugged ground made the operations of the enemy cavalry
less effective. More importantly the willingness of Pompey,
with a numerically superior army, to be hemmed in by the
enemy would be a public humiliation, perhaps weakening
the loyalty of his allies. Pompey replied by beginning his
own line of fortifications parallel to Caesar's. There was
considerable skirmishing between the two sides as they
fought for possession of key positions or simply to hinder
each other's progress. Pompey's more numerous army had
the advantage of being on the inside and so having to

build a shorter line, which eventually measured only some 15 miles to the more than 17 miles of the Caesarean works. In effect two armies were conducting a siege instead of the more normal forms of open warfare which, for Caesar's forces, were reminiscent of some of their conflict in Gaul.

Both armies, and especially the Caesareans, were on very short rations, but Pompey's army had a very large number of animals, both cavalry mounts and baggage animals, which began to suffer. Priority went to the cavalry and soon pack and draught animals were dying in great numbers. Caesar managed to dam the streams that carried water into the enemy positions. For a while Pompey's men survived by digging wells, but these did not really provide sufficient quantities and after a while the bulk of his cavalry and their mounts were shipped out. In the meantime, Caesar's legionaries dreamed of ripening crops and survived by eating barley rather than wheat, consuming far more meat than usual, and using a local root called charax to make a kind of bread. On seeing an example of this bread, Pompey is said to have declared that they were fighting beasts and not men.

The work went on as each side extended its fortifications further and further south. Pompey's army mounted a heavy attack which was easily repulsed by the troops led by Publius Sulla (nephew of the dictator Sulla). The enemy retreat was so precipitate that some of Caesar's officers felt that an immediate all-out attack might have won the war there and then. However, Caesar was not present and praised Sulla for not going beyond his orders, feeling that such an important change of plan was the responsibility of the commander, not that of a subordinate or legate. On the same day a series of diversionary assaults were also made in some force. All failed at the cost of some 2,000 casualties, but especially heavy fighting occurred around a small fort held by three of Caesar's cohorts under Volcatius Tullus. Heavily outnumbered, the defenders suffered many wounds from the vast number of missiles shot into the camp by the hordes of slingers and archers supporting the attacking legion. Nearly all the defenders were wounded, four out

NEXT PAGES
Warfare was usually seasonal so that armies could draw food and fodder off the land. Depriving the enemy of food was known as 'kicking him in the gut'. (Author)

of six centurions in one cohort losing their eyes, but somehow they held on. Caesar rewarded his officers and men lavishly, and they were granted extra rations, which at the time may have seemed even more satisfying than promotions and medals.

Soon after this success, two Gallic chieftains, Roucillus and Egus, defected to Pompey, along with their closest followers. Caesar claims that they had been caught claiming pay for non-existent cavalrymen and feared punishment. The desertion raised enemy morale and provided Pompey with considerable intelligence about Caesar's dispositions. Using this information, he planned a powerful attack on an incomplete section at the southern end of Caesar's fortifications, the main body striking from his own lines, while detachments of light troops were taken by sea and landed behind the enemy. The attack achieved some initial success, but as Antony and then Caesar himself led up reserves the tide was turned and the enemy driven back. To regain the initiative, Caesar replied with a heavy counter-attack against a camp originally built by Legio IX, subsequently abandoned and now occupied by the enemy. His troops moved through dead ground and woodland and achieved initial surprise, breaking into the camp, but then things began to go wrong. One of the attacking columns got lost, mistaking another wall for the rampart of the camp and following it towards the sea. Pompey shifted reserves to the area. The leading attackers began to flee and the panic spread rapidly as most of the 33 cohorts involved dissolved into rout. Caesar tried to stop standard bearers as they fled past him – a common gesture used by Roman commanders to rally their men – but all rushed on, some leaving the standard in his hands, and one even trying to stab him with its butt-spike, prompting a bodyguard to slice off the man's arm. Losses amounted to over 960 men and 32 tribunes and centurions killed and more taken prisoner. Fortunately, Pompey failed to follow up his advantage so soon after the failure of his own attack, prompting Caesar to declare that he would have lost if only the enemy commander had known how to win. Labienus was allowed to take charge of the prisoners and had them all executed. Parading his army, Caesar publicly punished several of the standard-bearers and tried to inspire the rest. Judging that their morale was at a low ebb, he decided that they needed to be encouraged before he risked a major action. Evacuating his sick and wounded, Caesar decided to withdraw, sending his baggage train out of camp at night to conceal his intention from the enemy. The main column was then able to withdraw with little hindrance. Only a few Pompeian cavalry managed to catch up with the retreating army and these were defeated by Caesar's cavalry, closely supported by a picked unit of 400 infantry.

Pharsalus

Caesar headed into Thessaly, hoping to join up with a detachment under Domitius Calvinus which he had sent to intercept Scipio and his two legions. His army began to recover its strength as the men passed through unplundered land and were able to harvest the now ripening grain. However, the reverse at Dyrrachium made some communities doubt Caesar's prospects of victory and the city of Gomphi refused to admit him or provide food. Caesar stormed the place and, for one of the very few times during the Civil War, allowed his men to sack the town. Some sources claim that the next day's march was more like a drunken revel, but also that the overindulgence appeared to cure much of the sickness from which many soldiers were suffering.

Pompey now had several options. One would have been to use his fleet to cross to Italy, now largely unprotected, but this would still mean that Caesar had to be defeated at some future date, and might be seen as running from his opponent. His personal belief was that they ought to shadow Caesar's army, but avoid open confrontation, hoping to wear him down by depriving him of supplies. This was a well-recognised Roman strategy, often known by the nickname of 'kicking the enemy in the belly'. However, there was massive pressure

Another scene from the Romanian monument shows a standard fighting technique. The legionary has punched his opponent with the boss of his shield and the stabbed him in the stomach. (Author)

from the senators with the army to bring matters to a swift conclusion by bringing the enemy to battle. In early August the two armies camped near each other on the plains of Pharsalus. Several days were spent in the manoeuvring and formal challenges to battle that so often preceded the battles of this period. The pressure on Pompey to fight grew stronger and stronger. Many of the senators were so confident that arguments broke out over who should receive Caesar's post of *pontifex maximus*, one of the senior priesthoods in Rome, as well as what punishment was appropriate for those who had supported him or tried to remain neutral.

On the morning of 9 August Caesar was preparing to move his camp to another position where the army could more easily find food, when he noticed that the Pompeian army had advanced much further from the rampart of their camp than was usual, and had come fully onto the level ground by the river Enipeus. Quickly, the order was passed for Caesar's men to take off their packs and then re-form in columns, wearing only the equipment necessary for battle. Then the army marched out and formed up facing the enemy. Altogether Caesar had 80 cohorts totalling 22,000 men and 1,000 cavalry. He formed the legions into the usual three lines, with the most experienced units on the flanks. Legio IX had suffered heavily at Dyrrachium, so it was combined with the almost equally depleted but veteran Legio VIII into a single command and placed on the left, next to the river. On the right flank was Caesar's favourite unit, Legio X. The entire army was split into three commands, Mark Antony on the left, Cnaeus Domitiius Calvinus in the centre and Sulla on the right. Caesar was free to move to wherever a crisis developed, but in fact was to spend nearly all of the battle with Legio X. The cavalry were all massed on the right.

Pompey's army was significantly larger, with the 110 cohorts in its three lines totalling 45,000 men and an enormous force of 7,000 cavalry on the left flank, supported by significant numbers of archers and slingers. Next to the cavalry were the two legions that had once served with Caesar, I and XV (now renumbered III). In the centre were the legions from Syria and on the right nearest the river the legions from Cilicia, plus some troops from Spain. The army was also divided into three commands, with Ahenobarbus on the left, Scipio in the centre and Afranius on the right. The main line was formed very deep by Roman standards, with each cohort deploying in ten ranks. Caesar's men must have been in four or five ranks, much closer to the

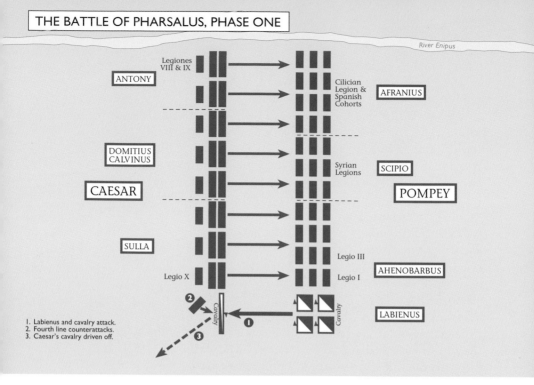

River Enipus

Legiones VIII & IX

ANTONY

Cilician Legion & Spanish Cohorts

AFRANIUS

DOMITIUS CALVINUS

CAESAR

Syrian Legions

SCIPIO

POMPEY

SULLA

Legio X

Legio III

Legio I

AHENOBARBUS

Cavalry

Cavalry

LABIENUS

1. Labienus and cavalry attack.
2. Fourth line counterattacks.
3. Caesar's cavalry driven off.

Roman norm. Pompey had also given his infantry an unusual order, telling them not to advance to meet the enemy, but to remain stationary and throw their *pila* as soon as the enemy came within range. Both of these decisions suggest that Pompey doubted the effectiveness of his own legionaries compared with Caesar's more experienced soldiers. Instead of relying on them, he planned to win the battle with his cavalry. Concentrated on the left flank, they outnumbered Caesar's horsemen by around seven to one. They would advance to open the battle, smashing their opponents and then wheeling round to take Caesar's infantry from the flank and rear. Labienus was in charge of this attack, and may even have devised the plan.

The enemy's deployment made the massive superiority of their cavalry obvious. To counter this, Caesar took a single cohort from the third line of each of his legions and stationed this force behind his own cavalry, probably echeloned back from the infantry line. This fourth line was concealed behind the horsemen and Legio X and

not observed by the enemy. Both armies were now ready for battle, though some delay may well have elapsed as the commanders encouraged their men. For the battle Caesar's army were given the password 'Venus, Bringer of Victory' and Pompey's men 'Hercules, Unconquered'.

The battle began with an advance all along Caesar's line. Most of the Pompeians remained in position, but their cavalry surged forward against Caesar's horse, which gave way. During the charge and subsequent combat the Pompeians seem to have fallen into some disorder, the individual squadrons losing formation and merging into one great mass. Many of these horsemen were relatively recent recruits and neither officers nor men had much experience of operating in such large numbers, but there was always a tendency for this to happen if cavalry became too crowded. Suddenly, Caesar gave the signal for his fourth line to attack. The legionaries charged forward, yelling their battle cry and sounding their trumpets, and then using the *pila* as spears. The result was almost immediate panic, which spread throughout the mass of enemy cavalry until there was a great stampede to the rear. The supporting light infantry were abandoned and massacred or dispersed by the legionaries. Pompey's main attack had failed.

Although Roman legionaries are famous as infantrymen, Roman armies made extensive use of allied cavalry and other supporting troops. At Pharsalus, Caesar was heavily outnumbered in cavalry. (Author)

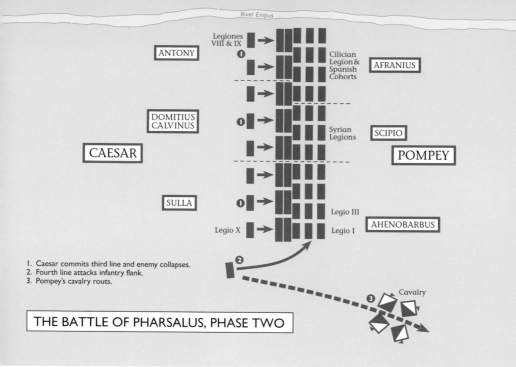

ANTONY

Legiones
VIII & IX

① ➜

Cilician
Legion &
Spanish
Cohorts

AFRANIUS

DOMITIUS
CALVINUS

① ➜

Syrian
Legions

SCIPIO

CAESAR

POMPEY

SULLA

① ➜

Legio III

AHENOBARBUS

Legio X ➜

Legio I

②

③ Cavalry

1. Caesar commits third line and enemy collapses.
2. Fourth line attacks infantry flank.
3. Pompey's cavalry routs.

THE BATTLE OF PHARSALUS, PHASE TWO

OPPOSITE
This Roman
gladius found in
Slovenia dates to
the 1st century
BC. Many gladii
had longer blades
in this era than
was usual under
the Principate. (©
National Museum
of Slovenia; photo:
Tomaž Lauko)

In the meantime the main infantry lines had come into contact. Caesar's men had begun their charge at the usual distance, turning their steady forward march into a run preparatory to throwing their *pila*, but had then noticed that the enemy was not moving. To prevent the cohorts from running too far, losing their formation and maybe wasting their missiles, the centurions halted the line. The nonchalance with which Caesar's men paused and redressed their ranks such a short distance from the Pompeians was another indication of their superb discipline. Reformed, the attack went in, the legionaries waiting until they were within 50 feet or so of the enemy before throwing a volley of missiles and charging, sword in hand, into contact. The Pompeians replied with their own *pila* – though it is doubtful if the men in the rear ranks of each cohort can have thrown their weapons effectively. A hard struggle developed, the second line of each army, which always acted as close supports to the first line, soon being drawn in. However, the fourth line followed up its success by attacking the exposed left flank of the Pompeian infantry, throwing that section of the line into disorder. Caesar gave the signal for his third line to advance and renew forward momentum in the fighting line. The pressure on the enemy was too much. At first the Pompeians went back slowly, but more and more units began to dissolve into rout. Caesar sent officers out to ensure that enemy legionaries were permitted to surrender, although his men were allowed to massacre the foreign auxiliaries.

Pompey had left the battlefield almost as soon as his cavalry had been swept away. He had ridden back to his camp, instructing the guards there to maintain a careful watch, and then gone to his tent. Later, as the rout of his army became obvious, he laid aside his general's cloak and left for the coast. If these accounts of his behaviour are accurate – and there must be some doubt, as they all come from hostile sources – his command at Pharsalus was remarkably spiritless, and his behaviour, being the first rather than the last to despair, utterly inappropriate for a Roman general. Caesar also claims that his men were astounded by the luxuries that they discovered in the Pompeian camp, items more suitable for effete Orientals than true Romans, although again this could well be propaganda.

Pompeian prisoners numbered 24,000, with supposedly another 15,000 killed. Nine eagles (the standard of an entire legion) and 180 signa (the standard of a century) were among the trophies. Once again most Pompeians were pardoned by Caesar, and he is supposed to have been especially pleased when his men brought in Marcus Brutus, son of one of his former mistresses and later leader of the conspirators who would murder him. Many other Pompeians escaped, but Ahenobarbus died in the pursuit. Some fugitives went to north Africa, but Pompey travelled to Egypt. Caesar's own loss

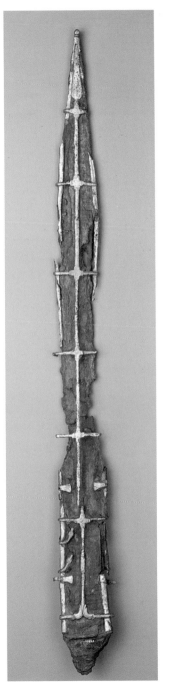

was comparatively light at 200 men, along with 30 centurions. Such a disproportionately high loss among these officers was not uncommon, the result of their aggressive and inevitably dangerous style of leadership.

Egypt – September 48–August 47

Caesar rested only for a very short time after the victory. Mark Antony was sent back to Italy, while Domitius Calvinus went with three legions, mainly consisting of former Pompeians, to Syria. Caesar himself took Legio VI, now reduced to a mere 1,000 men, another legion mustering some 1,400 men, and 800 cavalry and rushed in pursuit of Pompey; until he had been taken or killed there could be no end to the war. News arrived that Pompey had gone to Rhodes and then taken ship for Egypt, hoping to receive aid in rebuilding an army.

Egypt was wracked by its own civil war at this time, for the old King Ptolemy XI Auletes (or flute-player) had left the throne jointly to his son Ptolemy XII – a boy of about 14 – and his eldest daughter Cleopatra. The boy king was dominated by his advisers, Pothinus the eunuch and Achillas the commander of his army, a force that effectively included two Roman legions which had been in the province since 55 and had largely 'gone native'. Pompey's ship arrived on the coast near Ptolemy's camp and he appealed to the young king for aid. Since the king was unwilling to support a loser and eager to win favour with the victor, Pompey was lured ashore and murdered, the first blow being struck by a centurion who had served under him during his Asian campaigns.

Caesar landed at Alexandria on 2 October 48, and was met by a deputation from Ptolemy that presented him with Pompey's head and signet ring. Caesar is supposed to have wept, distraught at the loss of his former friend and missing the opportunity of pardoning him. This emotion may have been genuine, as indeed may his alleged desire to spare Pompey, but it is equally possible that he simply wished to distance himself from

the cruelty of an act from which he derived political benefit. Nevertheless he gave honourable burial to Pompey's remains, the tomb surviving to be desecrated by Jewish rebels in the 2nd century AD. Preceded by his lictors – the attendants carrying the fasces, the bundle of rods and an axe that symbolised the power of Roman magistrates – Caesar marched in great pomp to the palace. This display enraged the volatile Alexandrians and provoked some rioting. Caesar's soldiers responded with force and, since the late king had recommended his children to Rome, declared that both sides in the Civil War should disarm and submit to his arbitration. Some time in the next few days Cleopatra visited Caesar. The most famous story is that she was wrapped up in a carpet or blanket and carried secretly into the palace by a faithful Greek attendant, before being unrolled in front of a mesmerised Caesar. Cleopatra was 21 – more than 30 years younger than Caesar – exceptionally attractive if not quite flawlessly beautiful, highly educated, intelligent, and with a fascinating personality. Thus began one of the most famous romances in history.

It was not long before Ptolemy's advisers felt that their cause could not compete with his sister's for Caesar's favour. Leading their army to support the mob of Alexandria, they besieged the palace, blockading Caesar's men for six months. His soldiers were close to panic when the water supply was cut off, but new wells were dug inside the compound and the crisis averted. Reinforced by Legio XXXVII, composed of former Pompeians, Caesar became bolder and attempted to seize the whole of the Pharos Island, on which the great lighthouse, one of the Seven Wonders of the World, was built.

The skill of his Rhodian captains and sailors prevailed in a naval action fought within the Great Harbour, and allowed Caesar to land troops on the mole joining the Island. However, things began to go wrong as the enemy rushed reserves to the spot. Panic began with the crews of some ships who had landed to plunder and then spread to the legionaries. The boat carrying Caesar away was swamped by fugitives, forcing him to dive into the water and swim to safety, at the cost of abandoning his general's cloak.

Ptolemy had been held hostage by Caesar from early in the siege, and after this reverse Caesar decided to release him. The lad claimed to be reluctant to go, then promised to end the war, but, once he joined the army, promptly led it back to fight the Romans. The balance of power had shifted in his court by this time; Pothinus, assisted by Ptolemy's other sister Arsinoë, had murdered Achillas and these two were the real powers behind the throne. In the meantime an army led by Caesar's ally, King Mithridates of Pergamum, had marched overland from Asia Minor to Egypt. Leaving only a small garrison, Caesar took the bulk of his 5,000 or so men, and sailed out of Alexandria's harbour to join his ally. Ptolemy's forces heard of this and attempted to prevent their juncture, but failed. In open manoeuvring, Caesar showed the superiority of his men over the enemy and in a rapid campaign trounced the Egyptian army. Ptolemy fled but drowned when the boat carrying him to safety capsized. Arsinoë was exiled to Italy. Caesar returned to relieve Alexandria.

The war in Egypt was over, but for more than half a year Caesar had been out of contact with the rest of the world. The surviving Pompeians had had time to regroup and the Civil War would drag on. Yet, even though the war in Egypt was now complete, Caesar remained there for two months, allegedly spending his time feasting with Cleopatra. At one stage the Queen is supposed to have taken him on a luxurious cruise down the Nile. Militarily and politically, Caesar's inaction for this long period makes no sense. Perhaps he had never had a clear plan for what he should do once he had won the Civil War, or perhaps he was simply exhausted and could not resist a time of rest in fascinating company.

Veni, vidi, vici – the Zela campaign

It was not until late May or early June that Caesar finally stirred himself to move. There was bad news from Syria,

This frieze from Mainz dates to the 1st century, but gives a good idea of the classic fighting stance of the legionary – crouching slightly to gain the maximum protection from his shield, with his left leg advanced and sword thrust underarm. (Photo By DEA PICTURE LIBRARY/De Agostini via Getty Images)

and he sailed there with Legio VI, leaving the rest of his army to garrison Egypt. After the suicide of Mithridates of Pontus, his son Pharnaces had been left with only a small fraction of the old kingdom of Pontus. Seeing the disorder caused within the empire by the Civil War, Pharnaces decided to seize once more the lost territory, and invaded the old heartland of Pontus. Caesar's legate Domitius Calvinus had marched to oppose him, but suffered defeat. Pharnaces celebrated his victory in brutal manner, torturing and executing his prisoners, and castrating large numbers of young Romans who fell into his hands.

The forces at Caesar's disposal were small, consisting of the greatly reduced but veteran Legio VI, along with the survivors of Domitius's army. These included a legion of Deiotarus's Galatians which had fled before contact, another raised in Pontus, and Legio XXXVI, which, although composed of former Pompeians, had fought well. Though outnumbered, Caesar characteristically chose to advance on Pharnaces, stopping five miles away from the enemy camp outside the town of Zela. In the night Caesar suddenly marched out and began to build a new camp on the opposite side of a valley to the Pontic army. On the next morning, 2 August 47, Pharnaces drew up his army in battle order. However, because the ravine separating them was steep, offering very bad going to any attacker trying to climb it, Caesar thought that this was simply a gesture of confidence, of the type commonly made by armies in this period, and so allowed his men to continue constructing the camp. He was amazed when Pharnaces led his troops down across the valley in a full-scale attack. The Romans were unprepared and hastily tried to put together a fighting line. Scythed chariots – all but useless against steady and properly formed troops – caused some losses among the dispersed Romans, before their teams were shot down with missiles. The fighting was long and bitter, but eventually Legio VI on the right flank punched through the enemy line and exploited the success to threaten the remainder of their army in the flank. Finally, the Pontic army dissolved into rout and the fleeing men were massacred by the vengeful Romans. The legionaries were so exhilarated that they crossed the valley and stormed the enemy camp, in spite of the resistance of its garrison.

Although the battle of Zela proved hard-fought, it decided the war within days of the beginning of the campaign. Caesar is said to have commented on how lucky Pompey had been to make his reputation as a commander fighting such opponents. Later, when he celebrated his triumph over Pontus, the procession included placards bearing just three Latin words: '*Veni, vidi, vici*' ('I came, I saw, I conquered').

Africa – December 47–April 46

Although the eastern Mediterranean was now settled, many problems had developed elsewhere during Caesar's absence. Cassius's behaviour in Spain had provoked rebellion, while in Africa, Scipio, Afranius, Labienus, Cato and many other die-hard senators had raised an enormous army supported by King Juba. There were also difficulties in Italy, made worse by the lack of communication from Caesar while he was in Egypt. Several of his supporters, notably the tribune Publius Cornelius Dolabella and Cicero's friend Caelius Rufus, had tried to rally support by advocating the abolition of debt and had had to be suppressed by Mark Antony, who was suspected of having acted too harshly and was replaced as the dictator's subordinate or Master of Horse (*Magister Equitum*) by Marcus Lepidus.

There was also another mutiny among Caesar's veterans, news made all the more bitter because the ringleaders this time came from his own favourite, Legio X. The older soldiers wanted to be discharged and others complained that they had not received the rewards promised once their labours were at an end. These were their public grievances, but boredom may have played as big a part in provoking the outbreak, for throughout history armies have been more prone to mutiny when they are inactive. Caesar arrived back in Italy just as the mutineers were gearing themselves up to march on Rome. His behaviour amazed them when he rode into their camp and addressed them and asked what they wanted. When they shouted out that they wished to be demobilised, Caesar declared that they were discharged and informed them that he would let them have all that he had promised once he had won the war in Africa with other troops. Already stunned, the veterans were horrified when he addressed them as Quirites – civilians rather than soldiers – instead of comrades. It was an incredible display of Caesar's charisma and self-assurance, for soon the legionaries and especially Legio X were begging him to decimate them and take them back into his service.

Caesar was impatient to embark on the African campaign, and spent the bare minimum of time in Rome before hurrying across to Sicily. Reaching the port of Lilybaeum with just one legion, only bad weather prevented him immediately embarking for Africa. Frustrated, he ordered his tent to be pitched on the beach as a public demonstration of his eagerness and confidence. This was in spite of reliable reports stating that Scipio had formed ten legions, supported by four of Juba's as well as many auxiliaries and 120 war elephants. Even when he finally did set sail on 25 December 47, Caesar still had only six legions and 2,000 cavalry. The operation was not well planned, the ships' captains not having been briefed as to where they should land, and this, combined with unfavourable winds, resulted in the fleet becoming scattered. When Caesar disembarked near Hadrumentum, he had only 3,000 legionaries and 150 horsemen. Perhaps his instinctive – and characteristically Roman – boldness was now verging on recklessness, or maybe the stress and exhaustion of so many years of command were taking their toll.

The *dolabra* or military pick axe was very important for an army that made great use of temporary camps and entrenchments. At a pinch, it could also be used as a weapon. (Author)

Yet Caesar proved just as capable at improvisation as he always had in the past. Messengers went back to Sicily and Sardinia and soon he had gathered most of his troops. On 3 January 46 he shifted the army's main camp to Ruspina, deposited his baggage there under guard and sent the rest of the troops out foraging. A few days later he led another similar expedition to gather food, taking 30 cohorts, 400 cavalry and 150 archers. The legionaries marched *expedita*, that is, without packs and ready for battle, although the term is often mistranslated as 'lightly armed'. This time they were intercepted by a strong force of enemy cavalry and light infantry led by Labienus, which was later joined by another force under Petreius. Time and again the Numidian light cavalry swooped down on Caesar's line, throwing javelins before they swung round and retired. The legionaries charged forward to catch their attackers, but the Numidians easily evaded the men on foot. Whenever a cohort attacked it was exposed to more missiles from the infantry skirmishers, especially against the men's unshielded right flank. Casualties slowly mounted and progress was slow as the column moved across the open plain. Worse was the effect on the morale of the mostly young soldiers in the army. Their enemy was wearing them down and they were unable to strike back; some began to lose heart. One story, which probably refers to this fight, tells of Caesar grabbing hold of a standard bearer who was beginning to run, turning him around, and saying: 'Look, that's where the enemy are!'

In the meantime Labienus was riding up and down along the line, hurling abuse at Caesar's soldiers in the rough jargon of the camp. An experienced soldier, who had once served with Legio X but was now with another unit, managed to bring down Labienus's horse with his *pilum*, and Caesar's old subordinate was carried from the field. The situation remained desperate. Now surrounded, Caesar stretched his cohorts out into a single line – a rare formation for a Roman army – and had alternate units face about, so that they could throw missiles or charge in either direction. They then charged

and drove the enemy back for some distance. Quickly disengaging, the Caesareans used this temporary advantage to march on towards Ruspina, until they were again attacked by a new force of the enemy. Going round the line, Caesar urged his men to a last effort. As darkness was falling they launched an attack against an enemy-held hill blocking their line of march, driving the Numidians off and giving the whole army time to withdraw. Another version claims that Petreius withdrew because he wanted his commander-in-chief Scipio to gain the glory of defeating Caesar.

Caesar became more cautious after this display of enemy strength, sending to Italy and Sicily for supplies and reinforcements. Later in January two legions, XIII and XIV, arrived, along with 800 Gallic cavalry and 1,000 archers and slingers.

Caesar now moved forward to besiege Uzitta, forcing Scipio to come to its support. In spite of Pompeian naval activity, two more legions – VIII and X – arrived and Caesar felt confident enough to offer battle outside the town, although the enemy declined. He also took

Numidians were famed as some of the finest light cavalry in the world, riding without saddles or armour, and relying for protection on speed and small round shields. (Author)

the opportunity of making an example of one of the tribunes of Legio X who had been heavily involved in last year's mutiny. This man, Avienus, had brought so many servants and horses, along with copious amounts of personal baggage, that he had required an entire ship simply to transport his household. Such extravagance was shocking at a time when Caesar needed every transport to be crammed with soldiers or supplies, and so he publicly rebuked Avienus and dismissed him from the army, along with another tribune and several centurions who were known to have been ringleaders in the mutiny.

Caesar was still having supply difficulties and sent out several expeditions, one of which provoked a large-scale cavalry action in which Labienus was again defeated. The enemy was also sending out detachments to gather food, and Caesar attempted to intercept two legions isolated from the rest. The operation failed and as it retired his army was harassed by Labienus and a strong force of Numidian light cavalry and infantry skirmishers. Once again his own shortage of cavalry and light infantry made it difficult for Caesar to deal with such attacks. He gave orders that in future 300 soldiers in each legion should march *expedita*, without their packs and ready for action. These troops operated in close support of the cavalry, forming a dense block behind which the horsemen could rally, rest and reform after a charge and so prepare to advance again. This tactic surprised the enemy and caused them to become more cautious. After a period of manoeuvring failed to provoke the enemy to battle and left Caesar camped in an area without an adequate supply of water, on the night of 4 April he led his army out and marched back to Thapsus. The town was still held by the enemy, and the threat prompted Scipio to come to their support, dividing his army into two camps some eight miles from the town.

Thapsus was not easy for an enemy to approach because a wide salt lake permitted access only across a relatively narrow plain from the west or south. Such restricted battlefields offered an effective counter to the numerous and fast-moving Numidian cavalry which might otherwise slip round the flanks of Caesar's army.

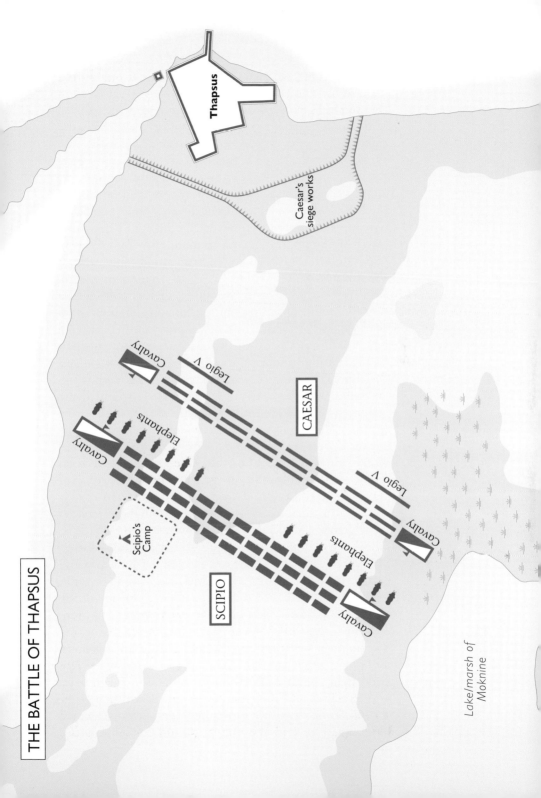

THE BATTLE OF THAPSUS

Thapsus

Caesar's siege works

CAESAR

Cavalry

Legio V

Cavalry

Elephants

Scipio's Camp

SCIPIO

Legio V

Cavalry

Elephants

Cavalry

Lake/marsh of Moknine

Even so, when Caesar observed that Scipio had deployed his army with elephants in front of each wing, he took care to strengthen his own flanks. The legions deployed in the usual three lines, with the veteran II and X on the right and equally experienced VIII and IX on the left. He then divided Legio V Alaudae (or 'Larks'), the legion recruited from Gauls, into two sections of five cohorts apiece and stationed each group in a fourth line behind the flanks. His cavalry and light troops were divided into two and stationed on the wings.

The enemy advance was sudden, and Caesar busily rode around marshalling his army and encouraging the soldiers. They could see that the enemy army appeared confused, and the more experienced soldiers urged Caesar to attack immediately, confident that the Pompeians would not stand. Reluctant to enter a battle before his army was ready, Caesar rebuked them for their impertinence and tried to finish drawing up the lines. However, a trumpeter on the right with the veteran legions gave in to the soldiers and sounded the advance. The call was quickly taken up by the musicians in the other cohorts and the whole line began to surge forward. Centurions desperately turned about and tried to restrain the legionaries, but Caesar quickly realised that it was now too late, so he gave the watchword for the day – 'Good Luck' (*Felicitas*) – and spurred his horse towards the enemy. This at least is the version presented by whichever of Caesar's officers wrote the *African War*. Another tradition claims that Caesar began to suffer an epileptic fit and this was the reason why the battle started in such a disorganised way.

However the battle began, it proved to be one of the swiftest of Caesar's victories. The enemy elephants were specially targeted by his archers and slingers, panicking the animals, which fled, trampling their own troops. Elsewhere the Pompeian legions gave way with very little fighting. The attack of the Caesarean legionaries was ferocious and they mercilessly cut down even those enemies who tried to surrender. The veterans seemed determined to end the war once and for all. Caesar's

War elephants were used by the Pompeians in Africa. At Thapsus a legionary of V Alaudae won fame when he cut the trunk off an elephant which had grabbed a camp follower. (akg-images / Erich Lessing)

casualties were very slight, compared to an enemy loss of many thousands. Cato committed suicide, as did Juba after he had fought a gladiatorial bout with and killed Petreius in a strange suicide pact. Scipio fled by sea, but drowned when his ship sank. Afranius, pardoned once before, this time was captured and executed. However, Labienus and Pompey's two sons escaped to Spain to continue the struggle.

Caesar went back to Rome. In the past he had held the dictatorship for long enough to hold consular elections, but now the Senate voted him into the office for ten years. He held four triumphs over the Gauls, Egyptians, Pharnaces and Juba respectively. Yet, in November 46, he had to leave for Spain to fight the final campaign of the Civil War.

Spain – November 46–September 45

Cassius had proved both corrupt and incompetent as governor of Spain, alienating both his own troops and the local population. By the time he was replaced by Caius Trebonius, the situation was almost beyond redemption and the new governor was expelled by mutinous soldiers. Pompey's elder son Cnaeus arrived and was rapidly acclaimed as commander of the rebellious legions. He was soon joined by other Pompeians, including his brother Sextus and Labienus. A huge army of 13 legions and many auxiliaries was raised, although the quality of most of the new units was highly questionable.

Caesar travelled rapidly as was his wont, covering the 1,500 miles to Corduba in just 27 days, and whiling away the trip by composing a long poem, *The Journey*. He had eight legions – the best probably being Legio V Alaudae which was experienced but still eager – and the old soldiers of Legio X, and 8,000 cavalry. The early stages of the fighting included a number of fierce skirmishes, but Cnaeus Pompey was reluctant to risk a battle. It was already proving the most brutal campaign of the entire conflict.

The Pompeians were suffering a continual trickle of deserters. Men accused of publicly stating that they thought Caesar would win were arrested. Of these soldiers 74 were executed and the remainder imprisoned. In the middle of March Pompey reached the hilltop town of Munda. Caesar followed in pursuit and camped nearby. The next morning, 17 March 45, he prepared to march after the enemy, but then saw that they were forming up in battle order on the high ground. Pompey had the bulk of 13 legions, a strong force of cavalry, and some 12,000 Spanish auxiliaries, half of them skirmishers. There was a level plain between this rise and the hill on which the Caesarean camp was located. His army marched out to deploy in the usual three lines, Legio X on the right and III and V Alaudae on the left, each flank guarded by cavalry. Once formed, the Caesareans marched down onto the open ground, expecting the enemy to do the same. The Pompeians did not move, keeping to the high ground so that the enemy would have to attack uphill.

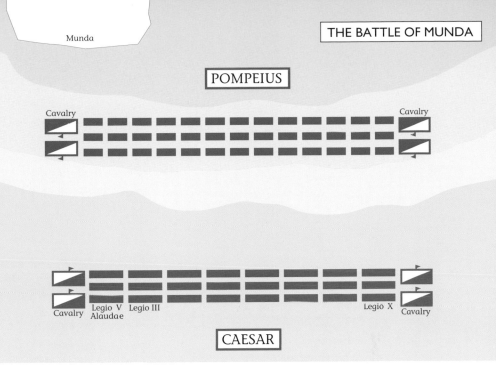

POMPEIUS

Cavalry

Cavalry

Cavalry
Legio V Legio III
Alaudae

Legio X Cavalry

CAESAR

Caesar's men were as eager as they had been at Thapsus and he attacked anyway, in spite of the disadvantage. The fighting was fierce and determined. One tradition claims that the Caesareans began to waver and that he dismounted and charged alone against the enemy, rallying first his officers and then the remainder of the army. In the end, the veterans of Legio X started to drive back the enemy left. Pompey tried to shift troops from his right to plug the gap, but Caesar's cavalry renewed the pressure on that flank and pinned the legions there. At last the Pompeians broke and were slaughtered in great numbers. All 13 eagles were taken, and most of the enemy leaders, including Cnaeus Pompey and Labienus, were killed in the next few days. Some 1,000 Caesareans had fallen, a heavier loss than in any of the earlier victories and testimony to hard fighting. Munda was blockaded, the legionaries grimly fixing the severed heads of Pompeians to spikes topping their rampart. The mopping-up took several months. Caesar had won the Civil War, but now it remained to be seen whether he could win the peace.

THE WORLD AROUND WAR

A Mediterranean war

The Civil War affected the entire Roman world and ultimately destroyed a centuries-old political system. Many ordinary citizens were swept up into the armies, to serve in brutal conditions. Some died in battle, many more probably through disease and privations, while others were permanently crippled. At least some soldiers, especially auxiliary troops such as Gauls, were accompanied on campaign by their wives and children, who in turn suffered from the rigours of hard journeys and poor food. Yet it was not just soldiers and their families who were caught up in the conflict, for many civilian communities also suffered. An extreme case was a town like Gomphi in Thessaly, which Caesar permitted his soldiers to sack in an effort to restore their spirits after the retreat from Dyrrachium. In such circumstances Roman soldiers were extremely brutal, impossible for their officers to restrain even had they wished to do so. Caesar deliberately did not march into Corfinum at night in 49 because he did not trust his men to keep their discipline once they slipped off into the dark streets, and he did not wish to begin the campaign by plundering an Italian city. In 46, it was also considered a considerable achievement when Caesar's men were camped outside Hadrumentum and he was able to prevent them from plundering it.

Communities within the area of any of the campaigns were likely to suffer even if they were not subjected to a sack. The armies needed food in vast quantities. Most hoped to gain as much of this as possible from willing allies or to ship supplies in from elsewhere, but this was not always possible, especially as operations became more protracted. The needs of the local population mattered little when the armies sent out foraging expeditions to gather up all the grain and cattle they could find. There were also cases when the armies clashed within urban areas, often causing damage. The siege of Caesar's small force in Alexandria brought considerable destruction on the city, as buildings were demolished or set on fire.

The Civil War pitted legion against legion and made Rome vulnerable to foreign enemies. The most spectacular success was enjoyed by Pharnaces, until his army was destroyed at Zela. Other threats failed to materialise.

Caesar's *Commentaries* talk a lot about the vital role of supply, and never is this more true than during the Macedonian campaign in 48 BC. Even so, he took a lot of risks. (Author)

Parthia had already invaded Syria once after its victory over Crassus, and seemed on the brink of doing so once again in late 50. Internal problems, during which the victorious commander at Carrhae was executed by the king as a potential rival, absorbed Parthia and delayed a new offensive. In the west, Caesar's conquest of Gaul had been quick and spectacularly successful, but the new province had not yet been properly consolidated. In fact there were no repeats of the rebellions that had broken out between 54 and 51 during Caesar's lifetime, but it did take another generation and further unrest before the province was fully pacified. Other allied countries sought to benefit from involvement in the Civil War. Deiotarus sent troops to aid Pompey in part because he was his client but also in the hope of securing his kingdom. Juba's attitude was similar. In Egypt the rivals in their own civil war tried to win favour from victors in the Roman conflict, Cleopatra gaining greatly from this and preserving some measure of independence for an area that had been in something of an anomalous position between ally and province for some time.

'Sulla did not know his political alphabet' – Caesar's dictatorship

OPPOSITE
On the Ides of March, when Caesar was assassinated, the Senate convened in one of these temples, part of Pompey's Theatre complex. Caesar's replacement for the Senate House destroyed in 52 BC was incomplete. (Wknight94/ Wikipedia Commons, CC BY-SA 3.0)

In the first years of the Civil War Caesar spent little time in Rome. In 46 he spent the greater part of the year there, having just been appointed dictator for ten years, and then after his return from Spain in October 45 remained there until his assassination on 15 March 44. The rest of the time Caesar was busy on campaign and ruled Rome through deputies. He was planning to leave once again to fight a war in the Balkans against Dacia and then to move east and confront Parthia in spring 44, a task which at the very least would have kept him away from Italy for several years. Yet, although he spent little time in the city, the period of Caesar's rule profoundly and permanently changed the nature of Roman political life. Caesar is supposed to have declared frequently that Sulla showed his political illiteracy when he resigned his dictatorship.

Evidently, Caesar did not plan to withdraw from politics and so the Republic would inevitably be dominated by a single all-powerful individual on a permanent basis, the very thing Rome's constitution was supposed to avoid.

However, it is much harder to say precisely what sort of position Caesar envisaged for himself in the long term. Civil war was renewed within months of his death, as his supporters sought vengeance against his murderers, and it was obviously in the interests of both sides to distort the record of what Caesar had done and, even more, what he planned to do. The conspirators needed to show that Caesar was bent on becoming an autocratic monarch who would have denied freedom to the rest of the Senate. Therefore he had to be killed because of what he would become. Caesar's heirs and supporters maintained the opposite view, pointing out that Caesar's rule had been and would have continued to be benevolent and that he had not wanted to become anything as un-Roman as a king. We have very few contemporary sources for details of the last months of Caesar's life, since most of Cicero's letters from that period were not preserved, and virtually all our accounts are later and inevitably influenced by the propaganda of both sides. Eventually Caesar's adopted son Octavian (Augustus) would make himself Rome's first emperor after his defeat of Mark Antony and Cleopatra in 31. As part of the adoption, his name became Caius Julius Caesar Octavianus. Therefore if either Caesar himself or Octavian passed a law, it would be recorded as a Julian law *(lex Julia)*, and if they founded a colony it would be a Julian colony *(colonia Julia)*. This makes it very easy to confuse the actions of the two men, and it is not always clear when Augustus actually implemented a measure that Caesar had planned.

Initially Caesar was given a ten-year dictatorship with the additional title of *praefectus morum* (prefect of morals). This was an invention that seems to have given him most of the powers of the censors, in particular the ability to appoint and expel senators and add names to the roll of citizens. In effect his power was greater than the consuls', and not only did he sit among the magistrates, but his opinion was always called for first. Even more importantly, he appointed all the significant magistrates. This provided him not only with control of the important offices of state, but also with the ability to reward the loyalty of his followers during the Civil War. The Senate grew enormously in size as Caesar's partisans were rewarded. By his death it had almost 1,000 members, compared with the 600 established by Sulla. Many of the new appointments were considered utterly unsuitable by traditionalists, for throughout the war Caesar's party had been seen as a haven for all the disreputable men and failures in the state. As Cicero joked grimly, how could you expect such men to guide the Republic when they could not even manage their own fortunes for a couple of months? Rumours circulated that in former years Caesar had gone round recruiting such wastrels by telling them that what they really needed was a civil war to restore their fortunes. Other appointments were unpopular, less because of the reputation of the individuals in question, but because of their nationality, for there were many aristocrats from the towns of Italy. In addition, Caesar, who had as consul granted citizenship to Cisalpine Gaul and during his campaigns extended the franchise to many noblemen north of the Alps, appointed several Gallic senators. This move again prompted caustic comments about barbarians, only recently bereft of their trousers and put into a toga, wandering aimlessly around the city as they failed to find the forum. Throughout his career Caesar had taken pride in always rewarding those who assisted him, and his actions as dictator simply confirmed this.

Sulla had filled his enlarged Senate with his partisans. Caesar to a great extent did the same thing. However, although most of the older and more famous senators who had sided against him were now dead, other, younger, men who had received Caesar's clemency were taken back and given honours and magistracies. Brutus and Cassius, the two main leaders in the conspiracy that would murder Caesar, had both fought against him in

49–48. Caesar appointed both men to the praetorship in 45. Yet all such honours were devalued by the freedom with which he doled them out to his supporters. The number of praetorships was increased to accommodate the number of men whose loyalty demanded a magistracy. The number of consuls was not increased from two, but Caesar encouraged men to resign before their year of office, allowing him to appoint others as suffect or replacement consuls. Such men were entitled to all the insignia of the full rank. An extreme case was Caius Caninius Rebilus, who had served as an officer with Caesar throughout much of the Civil War. When one of the consuls for 45 died on the last day of his office, Caesar appointed Caninius to hold a suffect consulship for less than 24 hours. Cicero quipped that he proved one of the Republic's most dedicated magistrates, never sleeping a wink while he held power, and that everyone needed to rush and congratulate the new consul before he had to relinquish it. In spite of this he, and many other senators, resented Caesar's disdainful treatment of the hallowed offices of the Republic.

At first Caesar was assisted by the dictator's traditional subordinate, the Master of Horse (*Magister Equitum*), a post held by Antony and later Lepidus. In 45 eight prefects were appointed to aid the Master of Horse, marking another stage between Pompey's indirect rule of his Spanish provinces and the use of legates and prefects by the later emperors to govern the empire. Though large, the Senate lacked any real freedom of debate and was becoming distanced from the main decision-making processes that tended to occur in private and involved only Caesar and his trusted advisers. If senators had, in 59 and afterwards, resented the need to go to one of the triumvirs if they wanted to secure any post or favour for a client, now the situation was much worse. It is possible that Caesar had become too accustomed to supreme military command to adapt his style of leadership to the more tactful needs of political life. He had spent most of his life for more than a decade issuing orders, which had always ultimately resulted in success. Caesar knew his own abilities, trusting them far more than he trusted the capacity of anyone else. His manner often suggested impatience with display and the feelings of others whom he did not respect.

On one occasion he caused offence when he failed to rise from his work and greet the consuls as soon as they came into his presence. The people loved the lavish games and spectacles he staged in Rome, but did not like his habit of listening to and answering correspondence while he sat in his box.

Caesar certainly displayed all the energy he had shown as an army commander during his dictatorship

OPPOSITE
Caesar had shown great favour to the communities of Cisalpine and Transalpine Gaul. In March 49 a law was passed regulating the legal arrangements of cities and towns in the Cisalpine province according to Roman principles. (akg-images / Nimatallah)

and the range of reforms he initiated during such a short time is truly remarkable. In some cases this consisted of tidying up an existing situation, as when he reformed the constitutions of the towns in Italy. The provinces too were affected, with renewal of the taxation system, usually in favour of the provincials. Plans were drawn up for a massive programme of colonisation throughout the provinces. This was to include not only the vast number of soldiers enrolled during the Civil War and now nearing retirement or no longer required, but also a significant number of the urban poor. Caesar had resisted pressure to abolish debt completely, the habitual desire of many citizens who lacked regular employment and lived in rented apartments, and arranged a more equitable system of repayment, but this measure would have eased the plight of many as well as adding to the number of prosperous citizens. It is uncertain just how many of these colonies were actually founded, for as mentioned above they are easily confused with the more numerous Augustan foundations. However, the programme was certainly already underway in Transalpine Gaul by the time of Caesar's death and had probably also begun elsewhere. Perhaps as many as 100,000 colonists were settled in Spain, Gaul and Africa.

The removal of part of Rome's population, which by this time was close to the one million mark, helped to relieve some of the city's problems. Laws were passed banning the trade guilds which men like Clodius and Milo had turned into gangs of thugs, although this measure may not have achieved much, as it still allowed 'legitimate' organisations. The number of poor citizens receiving a handout of wheat purchased and distributed by the state was reduced by more than half to only 150,000 recipients, many of those removed from the list being sent out as colonists. As a further measure to improve the food supply to the city, Caesar ordered the construction of a massive new harbour at Ostia, but this does not appear to have moved beyond the planning stage. A major building programme was begun in Rome, with older temples and public buildings being heavily restored and new monuments built. An entire forum complex, the Forum Julium, containing a new Senate House or curia to replace the one burnt down by Clodius' supporters, was begun. Occupying a prominent place within the complex was a grand temple dedicated to his divine ancestor, Venus Genetrix. Apart from making the city more splendid, projects such as this provided work for large numbers of the urban poor who might otherwise be a source of instability.

Apart from the grand parades that marked Caesar's triumphs in 46 and 45, he held many spectacular public entertainments, and in particular gladiatorial displays. On a more cultural note, a large public library was planned, supervised by the polymath (wide-ranging scholar) Varro. Caesar seems to have interested himself in practically everything, and probably his most enduring measure was the reform of the calendar. The traditional Roman calendar required constant attention from the priests, and had long since ceased to conform to the natural season, creating problems for Rome's political year. Caesar replaced this with a calendar of twelve 30-day solar months. In 46, 67 days were added to the year so that the new calendar would begin at the right time. The modern Gregorian calendar, created in the late 16th century and slowly adopted throughout the world, modified Caesar's system but left it substantially intact. The month of July still bears the name of the Roman dictator.

HOW THE WAR ENDED

The Ides of March

On 15 February 44, Caesar's dictatorship and other powers were extended for life. A month later he was stabbed to death by a group of senators that included men who had served him for years, as well as pardoned Pompeians. Before discussing why the conspirators acted in this way, we must consider the difficult question of Caesar's own long-term aims – a subject of continuing scholarly debate and little agreement. It has often been stated that the Roman Republic failed and was replaced by the rule of emperors because the system, designed to regulate the public affairs of a city-state, could not cope with the changed circumstances of governing a world empire. There is some truth in this as we have seen, for during the last years of the Republic it became increasingly difficult to accommodate and regulate the competition between a few overwhelmingly powerful individuals. At the same time the Senate failed to acknowledge the emergence of a professional army or to do anything to provide for discharged soldiers who were no longer men of property, encouraging them to a closer bond with generals who offered them more. Yet, even under the empire, the institutions of Rome were to a great extent those of a city-state, but the emperors imposed more control of the system and encouraged the integration of first Italy and then the provinces.

Institutions developed to support a permanent army, kept loyal to the emperor alone. Senators still held most of the senior positions in imperial government, although usually with authority delegated from the emperor, but the number of people, both citizen and non-citizen, benefiting from the regime was greatly increased. The empire, or Principate as it is more often known, gave Rome and the provinces a remarkable level of stability, broken only twice by civil war in the first two centuries of its existence, in comparison to the period from 133 BC to 31 BC.

Augustus was Caesar's adopted heir, had risen to power as his father's avenger, and copied some of Caesar's innovations to create the Principate, although in other respects he learned from the dictator's mistakes and did things very differently. The Roman Republic faced many political, social, economic and military problems in the 1st century, and it is worth considering to what extent Caesar was aware of these. He had fought the Civil War to maintain his own honour and political status. Had a compromise been reached that permitted him to stand for a second consulship and go on to a further provincial command, the future would have been very different, with Rome dominated by two great men, Caesar and Pompey, instead of just one. This did not occur and, whether or not Caesar had long aimed at supreme power, he did achieve it through his victory. His reforms as dictator were wide ranging, but did they have the coherence of a clear plan to solve Rome's problems, whether or not the solutions in themselves were practical?

There are essentially two ways of viewing Caesar. The first is to see him as a man perceptive enough to understand that the Republican constitution could no longer function. Throughout his career he had taken considerable interest in the conditions of the poor in Rome and the native population in Rome's provinces, and realised that the territories could not be run simply for the selfish benefit of a tiny elite in Rome. Observing the incompetence and weakness of the Senate as a group

NEXT PAGES
Augustus began his career as the heir and avenger of Caesar. Later, he made the Temple of Mars the Avenger the centrepiece of his new Forum complex. (Author)

and of individual senators, and contrasting this with his own abilities, Caesar knew that the state needed to be guided by a single individual who could discern the general good and act accordingly. In this way he tried to bring to Rome the stability it would gain from the Principate, and failed only because the Romans were not yet ready for this revolution; and perhaps because he let his impatience show. If Caesar thought in this way, then he may not have been entirely unique. On several occasions Cicero had talked of the need for the Republic to have a rector, a powerful leader who would help to guide the Senate and magistrates in making decisions for the common good. He had hoped that Pompey might fulfil this role, but even at his most optimistic had lower expectations for Caesar. Cicero's rector was certainly a less powerful figure than the dictator Caesar had become.

The alternative is to see Caesar more as an aristocrat steeped in the traditions of the Senate than as a visionary. Caesar, like all men of his class and upbringing, wished to have a distinguished public career, holding high office and winning fame and glory on the state's behalf. Perhaps because his family had for generations been removed from the inner circle of the Senate, or perhaps just because he was aware of his own great gifts, his ambition was especially great, and he not only wished to succeed, but to achieve more than anyone else. This is the man who is supposed to have said that it would be harder to push him down from first to second place in the state than from second to last. He pursued his ambition with relentless purpose, adopting any radical measure to achieve his ends, even to the extent of fighting a civil war. By 45 Caesar had achieved his objective, for all potential rivals were dead and he was able to celebrate more and greater triumphs than any other Roman, permanently commemorating his achievements in a massive building programme. That he now had supreme authority in the state and the ability to reform the Republic was largely incidental. There was no grand plan for solving Rome's problems, for Caesar was either unaware of them or

OPPOSITE
This bust was found near Roman Arleta (Arles in Southern France). It may depict Caesar or a local worthy who wanted to be depicted as looking like the famous victor. (Photo by Chris Hellier/Corbis via Getty Images)

could not think of any way of solving them. Instead he wasted his energy with huge numbers of unconnected initiatives and reforms, tinkering with minor problems rather than confronting the real issues. It was not long before he wished again for the simple objectives of an army commander, and so decided to leave his political problems behind and instead go and fight long wars in Dacia and Parthia.

We do not know what Caesar's long-term plans were, and the contradictory propaganda of both sides after his death will probably forever make these uncertain. Perhaps he was a mixture of the two extremes. Certainly there is no evidence that he planned ever to resign his considerable powers, but whether he thought of these as personal, or planned to create a permanent position of dictator, emperor or king and to pass this on to a successor is impossible to state with certainty. At the time many Romans certainly feared that this would happen, and at least some of the conspirators thought that they were striking a blow for liberty, in the sense of desiring that Roman aristocrats had freedom to pursue their political careers without the supervision of one all-powerful individual.

Brutus, one of the leaders of the conspiracy and the man felt by all to have had the most altruistic motives, certainly acted because he feared what Caesar might become. Married to the daughter of Cato, and a learned and serious student of philosophy himself, Brutus objected to the idea of a dictator or king, but did not hate Caesar. Caesar was indeed very fond of Brutus, and had once had an affair with his mother, the lively and intelligent Servilia, whom he appears to have regarded far more highly than any of his other mistresses with the exception of Cleopatra. This relationship prompted rumours, undoubtedly false but no less persistent for all that, that Brutus was in fact Caesar's illegitimate son. Others among the conspiracy acted more from personal hatred, or in the case of his former officers, who included Decimus Brutus and Caius Trebonius, disappointment with their rewards.

OPPOSITE
Brutus, Shakespeare's 'noblest Roman of them all', was falsely rumoured to be Caesar's illegitimate son. More than any of the other conspirators, he believed sincerely in their cause. (Bettmann via Getty Images)

Caesar had already been voted many exceptional honours, not unprecedented but usually on a grander scale than any of his predecessors. Caesar's link with the goddess Venus seemed to be more public and was represented as closer than the claims of past commanders, such as Sulla and Pompey, to be especially favoured by the gods. A temple was dedicated to Caesar's Clementia, the clemency with which he had pardoned so many of his bitter enemies. In public Caesar was granted the right always to wear a laurel wreath – an honour which is said to have especially pleased him for he was concerned over his growing baldness – as well as the robes of a triumphing general, and he sat on a gilded chair instead of the magistrate's simpler seat. Rumours abounded that he wished to go a stage further and become a king, perhaps after the model of the Hellenistic world where the monarch was considered to be a god. When a crowd hailed him as *rex* (king), he replied that he was 'Not Rex, but Caesar' for Rex was also a family name in Rome. Later he made great show of refusing a crown offered to him by the mob.

Yet his behaviour gave sufficient grounds for doubting his long-term intentions. He dressed in the long-sleeved tunic and high boots of the kings of Alba Longa, a long-vanished city that had been a rival of early Rome, and from the royal family of which the Julii Caesares claimed descent. Caesar, having lost his only legitimate child, Julia, had already adopted his nephew Octavian as his heir, sending the teenager to Greece to prepare for the eastern expedition, but it was not clear whether he was to inherit just his private possessions or also his position. Even more worryingly, Cleopatra had come to Italy and been openly installed in a big house as Caesar's mistress. A statue of the Egyptian queen was placed next to that of the goddess in Caesar's great temple to Venus. Wild rumours circulated about special legislation being planned to permit Caesar to marry her. After Caesar's death a boy was produced by the queen and Mark Antony, who claimed that he was Caesar's illegitimate son and named him Caesarion, claiming

OPPOSITE
This huge relief on the Temple of Dendera in Egypt depicts Cleopatra and Caesarion in the traditional garb and pose of the ancient pharaohs. Caesarion was only an infant when this was made. (iStock)

that the dictator had acknowledged him. There is no contemporary record of the child dating to before March 44, and considerable doubt must exist as to his actual paternity. Another rumour current at the time spoke of an ancient prophecy, part of the Sybilline Books that had often guided the Republic at times of crisis, which declared that Parthia would only be conquered by a king. The Senate is supposed to have been planning a decree that would grant Caesar the title throughout the empire but not in Italy itself. Yet, whatever his ambitions Caesar made no attempt to rule by force, dismissing his personal bodyguard and travelling through the streets of Rome just like any other senator.

Caesar planned to leave Rome on 18 March 44 and, given the scale of his planned campaigns, would be most unlikely to return for several years. Brutus, Cassius and the more than 60 other conspirators decided that they must act. They were a disparate group, but had preserved their secret for several months. On the morning of 15 March (a date known as the Ides) there was some dismay when Caesar did not arrive at the Senate on time. Eventually he came and the Senate rose to greet him. The conspirators clustered round his chair, using the excuse of pleading for the recall of Publius Cimber. For a while the charade went on, but when Caesar stood to leave and tried to shake them off, the conspirators drew their knives, Casca striking the first blow from behind. Caesar died of multiple stab wounds. There was a final irony about his death, for Caesar's own Senate House had not been completed and the old *curia* still lay in ruins from its destruction by Clodius's men. As a result, the Senate had assembled in a temple attached to Pompey's theatre complex. When Caesar fell, his body lay at the foot of a statue of Pompey.

CONCLUSIONS AND CONSEQUENCES

Civil wars and the end of the Republic

At Brutus' insistence the conspirators killed only Caesar. Mark Antony threw off his senator's toga to escape, not realising that he was not in danger, mingling with the crowd as the senators fled in panic. No one seems to have had much idea of what was going to happen next. Slowly and cautiously, apparently realising that there were not gangs of supporters bent on revolution and pillage, the Senate went back to the Capitol and spoke to the conspirators. The value of Brutus' reputation to the conspirators was now proved, for the vast majority of the senators were ready to listen to him. The more distinguished members, including Cicero, stood with the conspirators, signifying their support and after a few hours even Antony and Lepidus, Caesar's most important subordinates, appeared to be reconciled to the deed. The reaction of the population as a whole was less certain, for Caesar had always been popular with the poorer citizens, and there was some open protest when Brutus made a public speech explaining their motives.

Perhaps the conspirators simply expected everything to return to normal. The dictator was dead, so the Senate and properly elected magistrates could resume their guidance of the state. The problem was that virtually no one could remember a time when the traditional institutions of the Republic had functioned properly. Even the oldest, and there were few enough of these left after the Civil War, had grown up with a world of dictators like Sulla and Caesar, the dominance of informal triumvirs and the ever present threat of revolution from men like Lepidus, Catiline and Clodius. Caesar's former supporters seemed willing to agree to a general amnesty for the conspirators. The latter made no demands for personal power, and although the leaders were soon given provinces, this was no more than their due as ex-magistrates. Brutus even granted Mark Antony's request to hold a public funeral for Caesar. At this ceremony Antony read out Caesar's will, which included sizeable benefactions to the ordinary citizens, and, sensing their growing hostility to the conspirators, roused the mob to demand vengeance against the murderers of their hero. Some of Caesar's soldiers were making similar demands and most turned to Antony or Lepidus to lead them. The uncertain truce between the two sides continued for some months.

This coin minted by the conspirators shows two daggers and a cap traditionally worn by a slave granted his freedom. But not everyone welcomed the 'Liberty' proclaimed by Brutus and Cassius. (American Numismatic Society, CC0)

A new factor arose when Octavian, formally taking the name Caius Julius Caesar Octavianus now that his adoption had been confirmed in the will, returned to Italy. Moving from Brundisium to Rome, he rallied a few of Caesar's veterans. He was just 19, but incredibly self-confident. Mark Antony failed to take him seriously, and anyway saw him as a rival for the loyalty of Caesar's supporters rather than as a useful ally. It was round about this time that he and Cleopatra brought the child Caesarion into the public eye, presenting an actual son of Caesar to counter the adopted heir. Antony soon left for Cisalpine Gaul, taking charge of an enlarged army – for part of the garrison of Macedonia was posted there – with which he was in a position to threaten

Rome. To those senators who hoped for a return to peace and stability and were broadly sympathetic to the conspirators, Antony was clearly the greatest threat to peace, for Lepidus was cautious by nature and unlikely to act of his own accord, even though he had command of the legions in Transalpine Gaul and Nearer Spain. Cicero had his last great moment of glory, emerging as one of the most distinguished of the surviving senators to dominate the debates in the House. At this time he delivered a series of speeches attacking Antony in a way that was vitriolic even by the standards of Roman politics. The speeches were known as the Philippics, for he modelled them on the tirades directed at Philip II of Macedon (Alexander's father) by the great Athenian orator Demosthenes. Octavian was seen as a useful figurehead, who would help to draw support away from Antony. Cicero is supposed to have said that they would 'praise the young man, decorate him, and discard him' (*laudanum aduluscentem, ornandum, tollendum* – there is a rhythm and double meaning to the Latin which does not easily translate). Yet Octavian was building up his power and rallied a force of veterans from Legio VII and VIII, and was soon joined by two more legions which were nominally under Antony's command but answered the call of Caesar's heir.

At the beginning of 43 Antony reached Cisalpine Gaul, but was resisted by the governor from the previous year and one of the conspirators, Decimus Brutus. Antony's army was superior in both numbers and quality and Brutus was soon besieged at Mutina. The Senate resolved to send the two new consuls for 43, Hirtius – one of Caesar's old officers and the man who had completed his Gallic *Commentaries* and possibly also written some of the books continuing the Civil War *Commentaries* – and Pansa to relieve Brutus. Cicero and the other senators decided to employ Octavian and his legions to aid them, giving the youngster, who was not even a senator, proconsular *imperium*, just as an earlier Senate had chosen to make use of Pompey and his private army in the 70s. The armies clashed in a confused battle

at Forum Gallorum on 14 April 43, and after a hard struggle the arrival of fresh units forced Antony back with the loss of two eagles. Pansa was wounded by a missile during the fighting and died some days later. The army moved on to Mutina and attacked Antony's camp. At first things went well and they broke in, but then Hirtius was killed in the fighting near Antony's tent and Octavian and his men forced to retreat. Decimus Brutus was released from siege, but Octavian had no desire to welcome one of his father's murderers. Brutus began to journey to join the other conspirators in the east, but was killed during the journey.

Both consuls had died within a matter of days, and Octavian was now, effectively, in control of three armies, altogether some eight legions, plus cavalry and other auxiliaries. Rumours circulated at the time and later claiming that Octavian had had a hand in the deaths of both his colleagues. He moved south and stood successfully for election to the consulship for the next year, though he was probably very aware that the Senate was attempting to use him only as a short-term measure. Now that Antony was for the moment checked, they could begin to discard him, and rely instead on the conspirators. Letters began to pass between Antony, Lepidus and Octavian. After a while the first two joined forces, and later in the year all three met at Bononia. Together, at the head of a huge army – altogether nearly 43 legions, though not all were present – they seized Rome and on 27 November 43 had a tribune pass a law by which they became triumvirs with consular power to restore the state (*triumviri rei publicae*

OPPOSITE
Cicero was the greatest orator of his day as well as a politician. His letters, published posthumously, provide a very vivid picture of the period of the Civil War. (Photo By DEA / A. DAGLI ORTI/ De Agostini via Getty Images)

LEFT
Caesar's image was very important in the rise of Augustus to power. This coin was minted in 43 BC and shows the head of the murdered dictator. (Ancient Roman. *Denarius (Coin) Portraying Julius Caesar*, 43 BCE. Gift of Mrs. William Nelson Pelouze, The Art Institute of Chicago)

Much of Roman politics occurred in plain view, reinforcing the idea that all citizens shared in the Republic. The speakers' platform was known as the rostra because it was decorated with the prows of captured warships. (Author)

constituendae consulari potestate) for five years. The wording was almost the same as the dictatorships adopted by Sulla and Caesar, save that this time there were three men instead of one. The need to avenge Caesar figured heavily in their propaganda, and the dead dictator was formally deified and a temple constructed for his cult. A comet seen in 44 was proclaimed as a clear sign that Caesar had ascended to heaven after his murder, and from now on Octavian was regarded as the son of a god.

There was far more of Sulla than Caesar about the triumvirs' behaviour, for this time there was no talk of clemency, and the lists of the proscribed were again posted. Some 200–300 senators and several thousand equestrians suffered death as a result. Among them was Cicero, caught by Antony's horsemen as he fled in his carriage. His head, along with the hand that had penned the Philippics, was nailed to the speaker's platform in the forum. Many of these men were killed for political reasons, but the triumvirs needed money to support their huge war effort and plenty of names were added to the list simply to confiscate their property. In spite of this they still had to levy extraordinary taxation. What was left of the Senate was packed with the triumvirs' supporters and simply confirmed, often in advance, their actions. Preparing for war, and also keen to cement their own power, they took provinces. Antony received Gallia Comata (long-haired Gaul), the area conquered by Caesar, Lepidus had Transalpine Gaul and Spain, and Octavian was given Sicily, Sardinia and Africa. Octavian was also betrothed to Antony's step-daughter Claudia.

Meanwhile, Brutus and Cassius had had time to prepare a large army, drawing on the provinces around the eastern Mediterranean just as Pompey had done. In the end they amassed some 17 legions, including some such as Legio XXXVI which had fought first for Pompey and then for Caesar in the last Civil War, and would now fight against Caesar's heirs. Cicero's son was with them, serving as a cavalry officer. Antony and Octavian brought 22 legions to oppose them in the summer of 42. They met in the twin battles of Philippi. In the first Antony routed the wing commanded by Cassius, who committed suicide without realising that Brutus had in turn smashed Octavian's legions. Various stories claimed that the latter had either fled in terror or been ill in his tent during this battle. A few weeks later the second battle was fought and, on this occasion, the Caesarean cause won an outright victory, Brutus emulating the action of his colleague. Most of the credit for the victory went, probably rightly, to Antony.

After this victory Octavian and Mark Antony began gradually to ease out Lepidus, who was transferred to the province of Africa, while Octavian took Spain and Antony Gaul. Afterwards Antony went to the east to ensure the loyalty of the region and to secure provinces still threatened by the Parthians, who had begun to become more aggressive again. The son of Labienus had gone into exile at the king's court, and led a band of followers as part of a Parthian invasion of Syria. At the same time Pompey's younger son Sextus, who had escaped after Munda, had built up a considerable fleet in Sicily and was actively opposing the triumvirs. He was a problem most of all for Octavian, whose task it was to supervise Italy. One of Octavian's greatest tasks was to arrange the demobilisation of nearly 100,000 soldiers, a mixture of captured enemies and men whose service was up or who were no longer needed after the victory at Philippi. In 41 he began confiscating land throughout Italy to provide farms for these veterans, evicting many farmers, including the poet Virgil. Capitalising on the resentment this caused, while at the same time hoping to win over as many veterans as they could, Antony's formidable wife Fulvia and his opportunistic brother Lucius publicly rallied support against Octavian. In the autumn they raised an army, but were besieged at the town of Perusia. Excavations on the site have produced many moulded-lead sling bullets fired by both sides, which often contain political slogans and even more frequently extremely crude insults. It was not until the beginning of the next year that Lucius was forced to surrender, but during this time most of Antony's commanders in the west showed their allegiance to Antony.

Missile-armed troops played an important part in the Civil War, especially during sieges and at the blockade of Dyrrachium. This scene from Trajan's Column shows a slinger. (Author)

It looked as if an open breach had occurred between the triumvirs which could only be solved by yet another civil war. Fighting began at Brundisium, but at the last minute the two leaders patched up their alliance. Fulvia had died of disease, so Antony married Octavian's sister Octavia. They confirmed the division of the empire, so that effectively Antony controlled the eastern Mediterranean and Octavian the west. A short-lived treaty was agreed at Misenum with Sextus Pompey, granting him pardon and acknowledging his power, but this was soon in ruins, since neither Sextus nor Octavian adhered to its terms. Antony busied himself with a Parthian expedition, while Octavian built up his naval power to confront Sextus. In 36, aided by squadrons sent by Antony, Octavian's admiral and close friend Marcus Vipsanius Agrippa defeated the Pompeian fleet at the battle of Naulochos fought off the coast of Sicily. Sextus fled to the east, where he was captured by one of Antony's officers and executed.

Octavian's military resources had been built up considerably to undertake this conflict and were now markedly superior to Antony's. An abortive rising by Lepidus in Italy was swiftly defeated, and Octavian for once emulated his adoptive father's clemency. Lepidus was spared and allowed to live out the rest of his life in comfortable retirement, retaining his post as *pontifex maximus*, Rome's senior priest. In the meantime Antony had launched a major invasion of Parthia, beginning the war which Caesar had planned. Despite initial success, his offensive bogged down as the enemy harassed his supply lines. During the subsequent retreat the Romans suffered heavy casualties. The war had been a costly failure, but Antony refused the aid sent to him by his wife Octavia, and instead publicly praised Cleopatra for her assistance. His affair with the Egyptian queen became more open, and they paraded both Caesarion and their own children. Over the next years the fragile alliance between Octavian and Antony broke down altogether. Antony's obsession with Cleopatra made it easy for Octavian's propagandists to depict him as a man

OPPOSITE
In contrast to Julius Caesar, Augustus gave a prominent public role to his family, including his sister, Octavia. From early on, there were signs of the creation of a dynasty. (Photo By DEA / A. DAGLI ORTI/De Agostini via Getty Images)

so dominated by a sinister eastern seductress that he had betrayed his Roman origins. His scornful treatment of the respectable, and Roman, matron Octavia only made this task easier. Octavian portrayed himself as the champion of all Italy (*tota Italia*) against the eastern menace. War finally came in 31, and culminated in Antony's defeat at the naval battle of Actium. He and Cleopatra both escaped to Egypt, and commited suicide shortly afterwards.

Octavian was now unrivalled master of the Roman world, commanding an enormous army of some 60 legions. Militarily, he was more secure than either Sulla or Caesar, but his actions soon showed that he had learned from the failures of both. When he returned to Rome in 29 he formally laid down his powers, dissolving the triumvirate. Eventually he created the system known as the Principate, but this evolved gradually and there were more than a few false starts along the way. At first his power was still too blatant, for he held the consulship each year, and there was resentment, especially whenever he left the city. It was at this time that he appears to have been planning to build an enormous palace on the Palatine Hill, with a monumental entrance approached along a new road from the opposite side of the hill to the forum and Rome's political centre. In time, Octavian's public position was made to seem less monarchic. He made considerable effort to disassociate himself from Octavian the triumvir, the man responsible for the proscriptions and other cruel and violent acts. Eventually he became, instead, Augustus, a name with deeply traditional associations, and the Father of his Country (*pater patriae*). When it was finally built, his palace was less grand, in appearance more like an ordinary aristocratic house, and was approached through the forum along a road lined with the houses of other senators. To all intents and purposes Augustus was a monarch, for his power could not be opposed by any constitutional means. From the beginning the Greek-speaking eastern half of the empire referred to him as king (*basileus*). Yet he managed to maintain the illusion that he was not the master of the state, but its servant, a magistrate like all other magistrates save that his authority, and his continued services to the state, were greater.

In its final form Augustus' powers rested on two chief elements. The most important, though the least public, was his 'power greater than any proconsul' (*maius imperium proconsulare*). Pompey had enjoyed similar, though not quite as extensive, power during his brief command against the pirates in 67. During his second consulship he had been granted a massive province embracing all of Spain and yet been allowed to remain in Rome and govern through representatives. Augustus was granted the same privilege, but his province was truly vast, including most importantly Syria, Egypt and the frontier zones on the Rhine and Danube. Like Pompey and others who had dominated the state, Augustus's power was ostensibly given to him by the Senate, and renewed every five or ten years, but there was clearly never any possibility of its being withdrawn. Every province garrisoned by a legion, with the sole exception of Africa, formed part of the Emperor's province and was governed by his representative or legate. In most cases these were senators, but Egypt, the supplier of a high proportion of the grain consumed by the city of Rome, was governed by an equestrian, for it was too risky to grant such a command to a potential rival. A new senatorial career – and soon also an equestrian one – emerged in which traditional magistracies, which remained prestigious even if they lacked real power, were mingled with posts such as the emperor's legate. Like Caesar before him, Augustus effectively controlled elections to all significant posts.

The other, far more public, element of Augustus' formal power was the 'power of the tribunate' (*tribunicia potestas*). The Roman people, especially the poorer citizens, had strong emotional attachment to the tribunes of the plebs, who had originally been created to defend them from the misuse of power by other magistrates. In this guise Augustus was the people's champion. Through it he was able to summon the Senate or the Popular Assemblies and could impose his veto. In fact Augustus

Augustus' house on the Palatine was styled after traditional aristocratic houses, but much larger as several complexes were joined together. Even so, as emperor he acted the part of one senator among many, the first among equals. (Carole Raddato, Flickr, CC BY-SA 2.0)

made little use of these powers, but he referred to them frequently, even numbering the years of his reign from the time this title was granted to him.

Ultimately Augustus' powers rested on military force. For the first time Rome received a permanent garrison. The emperor had his Praetorian Guard, and also formed a police force (the Urban Cohorts) and fire brigade (the Vigiles). All of these troops were kept directly under his personal control. He also took great care to ensure the loyalty of the army. Service conditions were fixed, as were the soldiers' legal status and rights. On honourable discharge each soldier was entitled either to a plot of land or a lump sum of money. This, along with the soldiers' pay, was funded by a special Military Treasury (*aerarium militare*) which was supervised, and often subsidised, by Augustus. The problem of veterans looking to their commanders to provide them with some form of livelihood was at long last averted, and Augustus also took care that the legionaries' loyalty was focused on him and no one else. The men were paid by the emperor, swore an oath of loyalty to him, and, when they performed any feat of gallantry, received medals awarded by him.

Military power lay behind the Augustan regime, but attention was rarely drawn to this. Most of the Republic's institutions persisted. The Senate was reformed and reduced in size to remove many of the less suitable men who had been enrolled in reward for dubious favours to the various sides in the civil wars. More Italians were included and in time senators would come from the aristocratic families of many of the provinces. Augustus attended the Senate as simply another member, if a highly distinguished one, pretending to be merely the 'first in the senate' (*princeps senatus*), an old and thoroughly republican title. He encouraged the members to debate freely and to vote with their conscience. Augustus may have genuinely desired them to do this, but in practice this was a sham. Every senator knew that his future career depended on the emperor's favour, and so the vast majority said what they felt he wanted them to say. Both the senators and emperor wished publicly to pretend that Rome had not become a monarchy, politely ignoring the obvious reality. From early in his reign Augustus began to groom a successor, although the appallingly high mortality rate within the imperial family meant that quite a few individuals filled this role. When Augustus finally died in AD 14, his successor, Tiberius, had his powers formally voted to him by the Senate and at first feigned reluctance to take on the role. By this time scarcely anyone could conceive of, or remember, life without an emperor.

Augustus succeeded where Caesar had failed. He had learned from his father's murder and tried to veil his power behind more acceptable titles. By 31 the population of all classes was also far more willing to accept the rule of anyone who could put an end to the chaos of continuing civil war. The Augustan regime was a very Roman form of monarchy. Through the success of his adopted son, Rome was to be ruled by 'Caesars' for centuries, for the name became synonymous with supreme power. Even at the beginning of the 20th century there was a tsar in Russia and a Kaiser in Germany, emperors whose titles derived from the family name of a Roman aristocrat who had made himself dictator and was murdered in 44 BC.

CHRONOLOGY

59	Caesar's consulship
58–50	Caesar's campaigns in Gaul
58	Clodius forces Cicero into exile
57	Serious rioting in Rome. Pompey called upon to supervise corn supply
56	Crisis in the triumvirate averted by meeting of Pompey, Crassus and Caesar at Luca
55	Second consulship of Pompey and Crassus
54	Serious rioting in Rome. Death of Julia. Crassus invades Parthia
53	Crassus defeated and killed by Parthians at Carrhae
52	Milo's gang kills Clodius
51	Repeated attacks on Caesar's position in the Senate. Pompey passes law requiring a five-year interval between holding a magistracy and being appointed to a province. Cicero sent to Cilicia
50	Curio acts on Caesar's behalf in the Senate. However, Cato and other prominent senators struggle to ensure that Caesar will not be permitted to stand for the consulship without laying down his command. Pompey's position unclear for much of the year
49	The tribunes flee from Rome. Caesar crosses the Rubicon and the Civil War begins. Pompey chased out of Italy, but able to sail with most of his troops from Brundisium to Macedonia. Caesar goes to Spain and defeats Afranius and Petreius in the Ilerda campaign. Curio defeated and killed in Africa
48	Caesar crosses to Macedonia. Prolonged stalemate at Dyrrachium eventually broken when Caesar retreats. Pompey brought to battle at Pharsalus and utterly defeated. Pompey flees to Egypt and is murdered. Caesar pursues him and is besieged in Alexandria. Beginning of affair between Caesar and Cleopatra
47	Reinforcements arrive and Caesar is able to break the siege and defeat the Egyptian army. Later in the year he moves to Asia and defeats Pharnaces at Zela. Caesar returns to Rome and prepares to campaign against the Pompeian army mustering in Africa under Scipio, Cato and Juba
46	African war ended by Caesar's victory at Thapsus. Cato and Juba commit suicide, and Scipio is drowned. Caesar returns to Rome and celebrates triumphs, but departs for Spain in the autumn
45	Spanish War ended by Caesar's victory at Munda. All 13 eagles

were taken, and most of the enemy leaders were killed over the next few days, including Cnaeus Pompey and Labienus. Caesar returns to Rome and establishes dictatorship

44   Caesar planning major Parthian expedition. However, on 15 March he is murdered by a conspiracy led by Brutus and Cassius. Octavian arrives in Rome and rallies support from Caesar's veterans. Antony given command in Cisalpine Gaul

43   Octavian initially fights Antony on the Senate's behalf, but later in the year they are joined by Lepidus to form the Second Triumvirate. They capture Rome and reintroduce the proscriptions, executing large numbers of prominent Romans, including Cicero

42   Brutus and Cassius defeated at Philippi

41   Antony visits Cleopatra in Alexandria and their affair begins (or at least becomes publicly known)

40   Antony marries Octavia

40–36   Antony's Parthian War

38   Sextus Pompeius wins naval victories over Octavian

37   Antony publicly 'marries' Cleopatra

36   Sextus Pompeius defeated at Naulochus near Sicily

32   Octavia openly divorced by Antony. Open civil war between Antony and Octavian

31   Octavian defeats Antony at Actium. Antony and Cleopatra escape, but commit suicide. Octavian undisputed master of the Roman world. In stages he creates the Principate, a veiled form of monarchy that will endure for over 300 years.

GLOSSARY

Afranius, Lucius
one of Pompey's officers who fought for him in Spain, Macedonia and Africa.

Ahenobarbus, Lucius Domitius
consul in 54 and a leading opponent of Caesar in the build-up to the Civil War. Defeated at Corfinum and Massilia, and finally killed in the aftermath of Pharsalus.

Antony, Mark (c. 81–30)
one of Caesar's subordinate officers, he was given both administrative and military posts. Emerged as one of the main leaders of Caesar's supporters after his assassination.

Brutus, Decimus Junius
cousin of the famous Marcus Brutus. Decimus served as one of Caesar's senior subordinates in Gaul and stayed loyal to him during the Civil War. However, during the dictatorship he grew disillusioned and joined the conspiracy led by his cousin and Cassius.

Brutus, Marcus Junius (c. 85–42)
influential younger member of the Senate who fought against Caesar in 49–48. Captured and pardoned, he was one of the leaders who led the conspiracy against him.

Caelius Rufus, Marcus
friend of Cicero, but sided with Caesar during the Civil War. The unstable Caelius Rufus then rebelled against him and was killed.

Caesar, Caius Julius (100–44)
maverick politician and brilliant commander, Caesar rose through civil war to establish himself as dictator. Murdered by a conspiracy of senators, Caesar's fame has nevertheless endured to the present day.

Cassius Longinus, Caius (c. 85–42)
having won a name for himself by defending Syria after the death of

Crassus, Cassius sided with Pompey during the Civil War. Captured and pardoned, he and Brutus led the conspiracy against the dictator.

Cicero, Marcus Tullius (106–43) the greatest orator of his day, Cicero was more a politician than soldier. He survived the Civil War only to be executed on Mark Antony's orders. Cicero's Correspondence and other writings provide a mass of information about the period.

Cleopatra (c. 69–30) queen of Egypt and subsequently mistress of first Caesar and then Antony.

Crassus, Marcus Licinius (85–53) the man who suppressed Spartacus' rebellion and later one of the triumvirate with Pompey and Caesar. Crassus mounted an invasion of Parthia in 54 and was killed the next year after the defeat at Carrhae.

Curio, Caius Scribonius reckless young senator who was bribed to join Caesar and defended his interests as tribune of the plebs in 50. Killed in Africa the following year.

Domitius Calvinus, Cnaeus one of Caesar's subordinate officers, elected to the consulship in 53 and 42.

Juba, King ruler of Numidia and Gaetulia, he sided with Pompey, but took his own life after the defeat in 46.

Marius, Caius (c. 157–87) a man of humble background, but great military talent, Marius reformed the Roman army and had a spectacular career, but also provoked Rome's first Civil War in 88.

Octavia sister of Octavian, she was married to Antony to cement their political alliance. However, he subsequently discarded her for Cleopatra.

Octavian/Augustus (Caius Julius Caesar Octavianus, 63–AD 14) Caesar's nephew and adopted son. His rise to power and eventual defeat of all rivals led to the creation of a form of monarchy known as the Principate.

Petreius, Marcus one of Pompey's senior subordinates, he commanded large forces in Spain, Macedonia and Africa, but committed suicide after the defeat at Thapsus.

Pompeius, Cnaeus elder son of Pompey, who fought against Caesar in Spain and was defeated and killed at Munda in 45.

Pompeius, Sextus younger son of Pompey and a gifted naval commander, he fought with success against Octavian until his final defeat in 36.

Pompey the Great (Pompeius Magnus), Cnaeus (106–48) Pompey rose to fame at a young age during the Sullan Civil War, forging a career which was as spectacular as it was unconstitutional. Joined with Crassus and Caesar to form the First Triumvirate, but, after the death of Crassus, relations with Caesar broke down and led to the Civil War.

Scipio, Quintus Metellus Pius Nasica one of Caesar's main opponents in the Senate, he proved an inept commander and was defeated at Thapsus in 46.

Sulla, Pubius Cornelius nephew of the dictator, he served as one of Caesar's officers, but died in 45.

Sulla, Publius Cornelius the dictator (138–78) the first man to lead a Roman army against Rome and the victor in its first Civil War, he became dictator and attempted to reform the Roman state.

FURTHER READING

Primary sources

The Civil War is well documented by the standards of ancient conflicts, but there remain many gaps in our knowledge. The best account is provided by Caesar's *War Commentaries* in three books covering 49–48, supplemented by separate accounts of the *Alexandrian War*, *African War* and *Spanish War* written by his continuators. The identities of the latter are unknown, but all appear to have been officers who served with Caesar and witnessed at least some of the events they described. All of these accounts are inevitably highly favourable to Caesar, even though in his own narrative he writes about himself in the third person, but they are very detailed. Another of Caesar's officers, Caius Asinius Pollio, claimed that Caesar did not always bother to check the details of events which he did not witness. Pollio's own account, written after Caesar's death, has not survived, although it is referred to in some of our other sources, such as the early 2nd century AD *Roman History* of Appian. Roughly contemporary with the latter were Plutarch's *Parallel Lives*, which include biographies of many of the main protagonists in the Civil War. Less useful for military detail, but invaluable for the political background and a vivid impression of the time, are the speeches, and particularly the correspondence, of Cicero.

Caesar (translated by J. Gardner), *The Civil War*, 1967.

Appian (translated by J. Carter), *The Civil Wars*, 1996.

Plutarch (translated by R. Warner), *Fall of the Republic*, includes *Lives* of Crassus, Pompey, Caesar and Cicero, revised, 1972.

Plutarch (translated by I. Scott-Kilvert), *The Makers of Rome*, includes *Lives* of Brutus and Mark Antony, 1965.

Suetonius (translated R. Graves), *The Twelve Caesars*, revised, 1979.

All of the above are also available as parallel-text volumes (i.e. with the Latin or Greek on one page and the translation facing it) in the Loeb Series. They also provide the most convenient version of Cicero's *Letters to Atticus* and *Letters to his Friends*.

Secondary sources

Adcock, F., *The Roman Art of War under the Republic*, 1940.

Bishop, M., and J. Coulston, *Roman Military Equipment*, 1993.

Le Bohec, Y., *The Imperial Roman Army*, 1994.

Brunt, P., *The Fall of the Roman Republic*, 1988.

Cowan, R., *Roman Battle Tactics 109 BC – AD 313*. Osprey Elite 155, 2007.

Dupuy, T., *The Military Life of Julius Caesar*, 1969.

Fields, N., *The Roman Army: The Civil Wars 88-31 BC*. Osprey Battle Orders 34, 2008.

Freeman, P., *Julius Caesar*, 2008.

Fuller, J., *Julius Caesar: Man, Soldier and Tyrant*, 1965.

Gelzer, M., *Caesar, Politician and Statesman*, 1968.

Gilliver, C., *The Roman Art of War*, 1999.

Goldsworthy, A., *The Roman Army at War, 100 BC–AD 200*, 1996.

Goldsworthy, A., *Roman Warfare*, 2000.

Goldsworthy, A., The *Complete Roman Army*, 2003.

Goldsworthy, A., *Caesar. The Life of a Colossus*, 2006.

Greenhalgh, P., *Pompey: the Republican Prince*, 1981.

Gruen, E. S., *The Last Generation of the Roman Republic*, 1974.

Keppie, L., *The Making of the Roman Army*, 1984.

Meier, C., (translated by D. McLintock) *Caesar*, 1995.

Morstein-Marx, R., *Julius Caesar and the Roman People*, 2021

Parker, H., *The Roman Legions*, 1928.

Roth, J., *The Logistics of the Roman Army at War (264 BC-AD 235)*, 1999.

Saddington, D., *The Development of the Roman Auxiliary Forces from Caesar to Vespasian*, 1982.

Seager, R. *Pompey, A Political Biography*, 1979.

Sheppard, S., *Pharsalus 48 BC: Caesar and Pompey – Clash of the Titans*. Osprey Campaign 174, 2006.

Southern, P., *Julius Caesar: a life*, 2018.

Strauss, B., *The Death of Caesar: The Story of History's Most Famous Assassination*, 2015.

Syme, I., *The Roman Revolution*, 1939.

Welch, K., and A. Powell, (eds), *Julius Caesar as Artful Reporter. The War Commentaries as Political Instruments*, 1998.

Weinstock, S., *Divus Iulius*, 1971.

Yavetz, Z., *Julius Caesar and his Public Image*, 1983.

INDEX